D0646580

eat *up* slim *down*™ Annual Recipes 2003

eat *up* slim *down*™ Annual Recipes 2003

150 Simply Delicious Recipes for Permanent Weight Loss

Edited by KATHY EVERLETH

RODALE

Eat Up Slim Down is a trademark, *Prevention* Healthy Cooking is a trademark, and *Prevention* is a registered trademark of Rodale Inc.

Printed in the United States of America
Rodale Inc. makes every effort to use acid-free ∞, recycled paper ♲.

"Discover Your Weight-Loss Personality" on pages 1 through 8 is adapted from *Outwit Your Weight* by Cathy Nonas, R.D., with Julia VanTine, Rodale Inc. © 2002 by Cathy Nonas.
"Pump Up the Volume" on pages 10 through 17 is adapted from *Dr. Shapiro's Picture Perfect Weight Loss 30-Day Plan* by Dr. Howard M. Shapiro, Rodale Inc. © 2002 by Dr. Howard M. Shapiro.
"Turn On Your Weight-Loss Hormones!" on pages 29 through 37 is adapted from *The Hormone Connection* by Gale Maleskey, Mary Kittel, and the Editors of *Prevention* Health Books for Women. © 2001 by Rodale Inc.

Book design by Leanne Coppola
Interior and cover photography credits for this book are on page 255.

Front cover recipes: Quick Cinnamon Rolls (page 202), Chicken Pesto Pizza (page 216), Old-Fashioned Beef Stew (page 106), Chocolate Cake with Fluffy Chocolate Icing (page 52), Pasta with Shrimp and Sun-Dried Tomato Pesto (page 122)

ISBN 1–57954–666–8   hardcover

2   4   6   8   10   9   7   5   3   1   hardcover

RODALE
WE INSPIRE AND ENABLE PEOPLE TO IMPROVE
THEIR LIVES AND THE WORLD AROUND THEM

FOR PRODUCTS & INFORMATION
WWW.RODALESTORE.COM
WWW.PREVENTION.COM
(800) 848-4735

Contents

Special Thanks

Sincere thanks and gratitude to all the supporters of *Prevention*'s Recipe Sweepstakes.

The generous companies that provided the wonderful prizes:

Capresso, Chantal, Component Design Northwest (CDN), Edgecraft, Hamilton Beach, KitchenAid, Kuhn Rikon, Tilia, Oxo, William Bounds, Wüsthof-Trident

The extremely helpful product representatives:

Gretchen Holt from Oxo, Kirby Kriz from Hamilton Beach, Brian Maynard from KitchenAid, Paul Ward-Willis from Wüsthof-Trident, Sam Weiner from Edgecraft

And, most of all . . .

A heartfelt thank you to all the enthusiastic readers of *Prevention* magazine and prevention.com who shared their superb recipes and candid weight-loss success stories. You are an inspiration!

Acknowledgments

Many thanks to everyone who contributed their time and talents in creating *Eat Up Slim Down Annual Recipes 2003*.

JoAnn Brader
Leanne Coppola
Kathy Dvorsky
Anne Egan
Cathy Fraschilla
Jennifer H. Giandomenico
Kathleen Hanuschak, R.D.
Robin Hepler
Joely Johnson
Joshua Lampe
Gale Maleskey
Jean Rogers
Kimberly Tweed
Julia VanTine

Introduction

Get ready to make more than 100 new friends! *Eat Up Slim Down Annual Recipes 2003* is the first cookbook in a brand-new series that brings scores of weight-loss winners—and their terrific recipes!—together.

Here at *Prevention* Cookbooks, we recognize that *Prevention* magazine and prevention.com readers are incredibly savvy when it comes to finding creative ways to slim down and live healthier lives. So we decided to create a Web site, eatupslimdown.com, in conjunction with the magazine so readers could share their wisdom. We invited readers to send us their secrets for shedding pounds, along with the delicious recipes they used to help them lose weight. They could also enter our Recipe Sweepstakes for a chance to win exciting prizes.

Inside this book are more than 150 tempting recipes for weight loss, including specialties of the *Prevention* Test Kitchen (they're the ones with the photos), and featuring 100 recipes sent in by readers. Your family will love these dishes, because families around the country are already enjoying them! Try Pasta with Veggie Sauce, a colorful, stick-to-your-ribs primavera; Sweet Maria's Salmon, so flavorful it'll turn meat-and-potatoes eaters into fish lovers; Chocolate-Raspberry Cooler, refreshing and satisfyingly sweet; and much more. You won't believe all the wonderful food you'll be eating while still losing weight!

We've also included "Three Ways to Win at Weight Loss," profiles of three of the hottest, most effective weight-loss strategies. We help you determine your Weight-Loss Personality so you can decide which of these plans—or combination of them—may work best for you.

Most inspiring of all are the success stories from weight-loss winners who have lost the pounds and kept them off: A new mother determined to reach her pre-pregnancy weight. A woman who gets exercise being a massage therapist. A married couple who lost weight as a team. And many more. You'll marvel at their perseverance, and you may even see a little of yourself in some of their stories.

If you enjoy entertaining, take a look at the menu section. A dozen ways to cook for a get-together—from a seafood supper to a backyard barbecue—and still stay on track with your weight-loss efforts.

Plus, sprinkled throughout are clever and practical slimming tips from readers that you can incorporate into your own daily living.

So take this opportunity to make new friends—and new recipes. Most of all, get ready to Eat Up and Slim Down!

Discover Your Weight-Loss Personality

It's the key to outwitting your weight. Pair it with these diet shortcuts and get *off* the diet merry-go-round!

If you're like 80 percent of women, you've been riding the diet merry-go-round for most of your life: up and down, up and down, each diet working temporarily but none seeming to stick.

Well, here's the truth: It's not just the diet plan you choose that determines your success. It's figuring out why you fall off and how to quickly get back on track that makes the difference. Once you identify your "food personality type"—the specific behaviors that set you up to overeat—you can more quickly derail destructive eating habits, stick to a healthful fat-shedding regimen, and lose weight for good by focusing only on the diet strategies that are right for you.

Check out the characteristics of the seven food personalities that follow and identify the one that most closely matches your eating style. Each personality has a colored icon that will help you choose which of the following 41 proven weight-loss tools will work to beat your specific eating triggers. For a shortcut to a slimmer body, pay special attention to the tips marked most helpful for you.

Figuring out your weight-loss personality will also help you decide whether other healthy-eating strategies presented in the following chapter, such as Dr. Shapiro's Picture-Perfect selections, the glycemic index, or a return to three square meals a day will work for you. Read on, and get ready to lose weight for good.

1

THE OSTRICH

You're most like the Ostrich if you . . .

- Generally think, "I didn't/don't eat that much."
- Often say, "I'll start my diet tomorrow."
- Avoid the scale, believing if you don't see your weight, you won't be your weight.
- Hide what you eat from others, thinking if no one sees you eat it, you haven't eaten it.

THE BABY

You're most like the Baby if you . . .

- Don't take responsibility for what and how much you eat.
- Tell yourself, "If everyone else is eating it, I want to, too!"
- Want what you want, when you want it.
- Overeat to be "polite." For example, "Aunt Lucy went to all this trouble to make my favorite lasagna, so I have to have seconds."

RESTRAINED EATER

You're most like the Restrained Eater if you . . .

- Seesaw between extremes of dieting and overeating.
- Always think, "I'll have just one."
- Eat like a bird in public but then find yourself bingeing in private.
- Frequently overeat diet foods, e.g., eating an entire box of fat-free crackers.
- Are always trying one diet or another.

SLOW GAINER

You're most like the Slow Gainer if you . . .

- Have poor impulse control.
- Don't know why the scale keeps inching up.
- Step on the scale with optimism and step off in shock.
- Bake for other people but taste and taste while you bake.
- Feel victimized, because you believe you're doing everything right yet are still overweight.

WEEKEND EATER

You're most like the Weekend Eater if you . . .

- Eat well and exercise all week but treat the weekends with abandon.
- Find that your biggest splurges happen from Friday night through Sunday night.
- Can't enjoy yourself if you have to monitor your alcohol intake or crunch calories on your Saturday night dinner out.
- Love to socialize and go to parties.

GOOD/BAD FAIRY

You're most like the Good Fairy/Bad Fairy if you . . .

- Use food as a reward and swear off food as a punishment.
- Ignore cheesecake in a friend's kitchen but then cruise your local bakery for a slice.
- Often think, "I've been so good. I never eat ice cream, so I can have some now."
- Punish yourself for overeating by starving yourself.
- Punish yourself for overeating by overeating even more, thus abandoning your weight-loss plan.

STRESS EATER••••••••••

You're most like the Stress Eater if you . . .

- Often feel anxiety, stress, or fear.
- Often zone out in front of the TV with a family-size bag of chips.
- Turn to food before anything else, including exercise, a hot bath, or a good book, to anesthetize scary feelings.
- Will reach for anything (powdered Jell-O, spoonfuls of peanut butter) when your favorite comfort food isn't available.

Find *Your* Diet Solutions

Focus on the tips that correspond to your food personality to permanently lose those extra pounds.

Play a game of "How many calories can I eat?"

Many women "awfulize" every slip, turning it into a diet disaster, which makes them give up. Make a list of everything you'd eat on your worst pig-out day. Now, guesstimate the calorie count. In the thousands? But thousands of calories might equal 2 pounds. So one day of overeating isn't a giant setback. Don't let it lead to a week or a month.

Tell it like it is.

If you tend to eat out of anger, try this trick to let out what's eating you: Write down why you're eating, what you're eating, and how it will satisfy you. For example: "My boss loads me with her work and expects me to stay late. I hate her! I'm eating this cake because I want to bite off her head." Ask yourself what would happen if you didn't eat. Chances are, you'll discover you can cope without food.

Use the tape trick.

Between meals, stick a wide strip of masking tape about chest level across the entrance to your kitchen. It's a very effective way to make you conscious of how many times you find yourself heading to the kitchen in search of food.

Beware "dunno" foods.

"Dunno" foods are those for which you're clueless of the calorie count, such as deli salads, mall foods, and ethnic dishes. They look innocent, but they can carry a bigger calorie load than you imagine. If you can't tally the calories, think twice before eating.

Cook when you don't nibble.

If you have to make potato salad for a picnic, bake cookies for a meeting, or prep for your dinner party, try to do it at a time when you eat the least, such as after a satisfying meal or in the morning.

Satisfy chocolate urges safely.

When only chocolate will do, try these (buy single-size servings; don't keep these foods in the house).

- Snack-size candy bar
- Small peppermint patty
- Fudge pop
- Frozen banana dipped in chocolate syrup
- Hot cocoa
- Chocolate sorbet with 1 tablespoon of chocolate syrup

Tally those little tastes.

Keep a food diary and record "tastes": a spoonful of this, a fingerful of that. Your brain won't register these eating episodes, but your body does. Some calorie tallies (1 tablespoon each): cake icing, 55; cream cheese, 50; peanut butter, 100; gravy, 40; sour cream, 30; a child's leftovers, 50 to 100.

Scale down the big four.

If you tend to overeat pasta, bread, rice, or potatoes, restrict them or omit them from your diet. You may lose a significant amount of weight. This isn't a low-carbohydrate diet; you'll still be eating cereal, beans, fruits, and vegetables.

Eat in two acts.

Divide the food on your plate in half (if dining out, make an imaginary line). Eat half. Now stop for 10 minutes; either leave the table or sip a glass of water until it's empty. If you're still hungry after 10 minutes, finish your meal. If you're not sure, divide the remainder in half and repeat the exercise.

Plan your splurges.

You can cut loose on weekends without letting go. Plan your splurges by saving 300 or so calories the day before you indulge. Then order that appetizer or dessert when you're out.

Delay your satisfaction.

Skip nibbling on tasteless low-calorie food. Allow yourself one after-dinner snack that you really, really want, such as a sliver of cheesecake. Then delay eating it for as long as you can. The longer you wait, the closer it gets to bedtime, so that'll be your one and only snack for the night.

Dilute your appetite.

Eating a small amount of a high-fiber or high-protein food an hour before a main meal helps some people reduce the amount they eat at the meal. Try 1 ounce of high-fiber cereal with fat-free milk or half of a small can of water-packed tuna.

Put your family on plate patrol.

If you scarf the scraps from your family's plates as you clear the table, teach them to scrape their plates directly into the garbage can and carry them to the sink or dishwasher. Then go on with your kitchen duties with temptation gone.

Don't eyeball oil.

Whether you drizzle your salad with olive oil or stir-fry your veggies in canola oil, measure it—always. That ¼ cup of oil you drizzle into the frying pan packs a hefty 482 calories. If you don't measure it out, you're bound to add a whole lot more than you think.

Close the "calorie gate."

Decide how many calories you want to consume in a certain prime binge period, such as 9 P.M. to 11 P.M. During that period, eat your fill of the lowest-calorie foods possible: bowls of cantaloupe, sweet peppers, steamed veggies. You'll be full but still well within a reasonable calorie limit.

Make a call.

Before you dive into that tempting cherry strudel you bought for company, call a friend and tell her what you plan to do. It'll help weaken your "need" to eat.

Order first, drink later.

Place your order before you have your glass of wine. Alcohol loosens your inhibitions, which makes you less careful about overeating.

Reach for control.

Wind a string or colorful bandage around one finger of your "eating hand" so you can see yourself reach for food. If you can see what you're doing, it will help you not to follow through on your impulse to eat.

Put your appetite on "disconnect."

When you feel like your eating is out of control, you need to disconnect temporarily from the activity of eating so you can decide whether you want to continue. Get up from the table and brush your teeth. Or stop and clean a room in the house. Do whatever gives you time to get a grip.

Think beyond cookies.

When making food for a gift, consider making healthy homemade herb-infused vinegars or salsas. Why make baked goods when you'll be tempted to sample them? (And the recipients may be struggling with overeating, too.)

Share a sinful entrée.

Dying for that forbidden fettuccine Alfredo? Ask a dinner companion to split it with you. Don't feel embarrassed. Chances are he might want to splurge, too.

Start low, end high.

Look at your plate. Pick the lowest-calorie food (typically the veggies). Eat that first to fill you up. Then eat the next lowest-calorie item. Save your highest-calorie food for last. You'll get a taste, but you may be too full to finish it.

Knock bread off the dinner menu.

If you love bread but can't seem to eat it in moderation, don't have it at dinner (when you're more likely to overeat it). Eventually, you'll automatically think, "I never have bread at dinner."

Buy single-serving snacks.

Cookies, chips, and even ice cream come in single-serving sizes. Eat a little container instead of a whole big box.

Divide to conquer cravings.

If you buy large packages to save money, use sealable containers to divide snacks into single servings.

If you can't beat 'em, join 'em.

If you can't resist finishing the remains of your children's macaroni and cheese or chicken fingers, have a salad with low-fat dressing for starters. Then have the rest of their dinner as your main course.

Follow the two-spoon rule.

At a buffet, don't put more than two different foods on your plate at once. Return as often as you wish, but each time, ask yourself whether you want more of the same, something different, or any more food at all.

Try the day-after tactic.

The day after you overeat, return to your weight-loss or maintenance plan. But for this one day, cut 200 to 500 calories from your daily allotment. Or add 20 to 60 minutes more exercise to help burn them off.

Picture a piranha in the peanut bowl.

At a bar, keep your hands out of the peanut bowl. They're 800 calories per cup, 200 per grab. Imagine there's a piranha in there waiting to bite off your fingers.

Cleanse your palate.

You can stop a binge in its tracks by making the switch to an entirely different food the moment you catch yourself in the act. So you've devoured half a bag of potato chips? Just close the bag and pull out a bunch of grapes or an apple. It'll let you break away from the junk.

Order from the invisible menu.

When you go to the same few restaurants again and again, you know the healthiest fare they serve. Order one of those dishes without even opening the menu. You won't be tempted by fattier fare.

Order by proxy.

Feeling shaky about your resolve? Have someone else in your party order for you. Then head to the restroom while the rest of the order is being placed.

Stretch your lunch.

If you get hungry in midafternoon, eat half your lunch at the regular time and the other half as an afternoon snack.

Try the two-meal tool.

On weekends, many of us eat breakfast late and lunch an hour or two later, and the meals are often bigger. Save calories by having just two meals: breakfast and dinner. If you get hungry in between, have a small, nutritious snack.

Assemble some 700-calorie meals.

Use a calorie counter to create dinners you can order in a diner or fine restaurant. One example: a glass of wine, shrimp cocktail, steamed veggies, broiled chicken breast, and small baked potato.

Factor in produce first.

Plan your food day by figuring the vegetables first. Add fruit and high-fiber starches such as brown rice and beans, then high-calcium food such as yogurt or low-fat cheese. Finally, add high-protein food such as fish, chicken, or meat.

Tout your smallest triumphs.

Celebrate any and all improvements you've made in eating. You're overeating less often these days? That's small win number one. You didn't finish that chocolate cake? Small win number two. Doing this will help you steer clear of all-or-nothing thinking and let you respect your progress.

Motivate with money.

Exercise and diet go hand in hand. You can help keep your exercise program on track by putting a dollar in a jar every time you work out. Then on the first of the month, spend your earnings on a massage, manicure, or other nonfood treat.

Eat what you love and pare down the rest.

Before you even enter a restaurant, decide what it is that you really, really want. Then go ahead and have it. The trick is to be sure to reduce your intake of other foods you can live without. For example, if it's pasta carbonara you crave, order half a portion, opt for salad with dressing on the side, choose seltzer instead of wine, and skip the bread basket.

Opt for eat-slow snacks.

Foods that are hard to eat take longer to finish, which gives your brain a chance to compute what's in your stomach. Try a baked apple, 4 cups of air-popped popcorn, two large carrots, an artichoke with low-fat dressing, or nachos with 1 ounce of baked tortilla chips, low-fat cheese, and salsa.

Munch in front of the mirror.

Place a mirror in your dining room. When you confront your image in the midst of a chow-down, it just might make you think twice about what and how much you eat.

Three Ways to Win at Weight Loss

Choose what works for you to become a weight-loss success story.

Once you have your weight-loss personality nailed down, it's time to look food squarely in the face and find a way to happily coexist. In the pages that follow, we introduce you to three exciting no-diet approaches to dealing with food and coming out a winner in weight loss.

The first approach, "Pump Up the Volume," is from *Dr. Shapiro's Picture Perfect Weight Loss 30-Day Plan*. Through the use of food comparison photographs, Dr. Shapiro shows you how to use visual cues to choose your calories wisely. The visual element eliminates the need to count calories, so this strategy can be especially helpful for those in the Weekend and Baby categories.

Next, "Weight Loss by the Numbers" reveals how the glycemic index system for rating

carbohydrates can help you shed pounds. It's all based on how carbs affect your blood sugar, and how your blood sugar can set off hunger alarms, causing you to overeat when you're not truly hungry. Restrained Eaters, Slow Gainers, Weekend Eaters, and Stress Eaters—who may tend to overeat or binge—may be good matches for this program.

Finally, we invite you to "Be a Square." You've probably heard of grazing—eating four to six small meals throughout the day instead of the three main meals so many of us grew up with. Grazing is still great advice for many people. But for others—likely, the Ostrich, the Stress Eater, or the Restrained Eater—it's an invitation to overeat. If this sounds like you, a return to the traditional "three squares a day" may be the answer you've been searching for.

Each of these strategies can work for just about any weight-loss personality type, but to help you find your way, each plan is color-coded to correspond with the specific personality types they match best. This is merely a guide, so you're not bound to any one strategy. Give them all a look, and decide what works best for you.

Pump Up the Volume

The secret to losing weight and keeping it off is to change your relationship with food. And it's a dieter's dream come true: Eat the things you enjoy. Eat until you feel full and satisfied—and still lose weight. It's not impossible when you learn to eat with awareness. You empower yourself to choose healthy foods that deliver the taste you love yet fill you up for fewer calories.

It's so simple. For a picture-perfect body, try Picture-Perfect Weight Loss. It's a concept that Dr. Howard M. Shapiro created in his best-selling book *Dr. Shapiro's Picture Perfect Weight Loss*. As founder and director of Howard M. Shapiro Medical Associates, a private multidisciplinary medical office in New York City that specializes in weight control and life management, Dr. Shapiro knows what works—and what doesn't.

What works, he says, is choosing to spend your calories wisely. In his books, photos

Week 1: Bountiful Breakfast

Think outside the box of Pop-Tarts and start your day with a hearty and satisfying low-calorie breakfast.

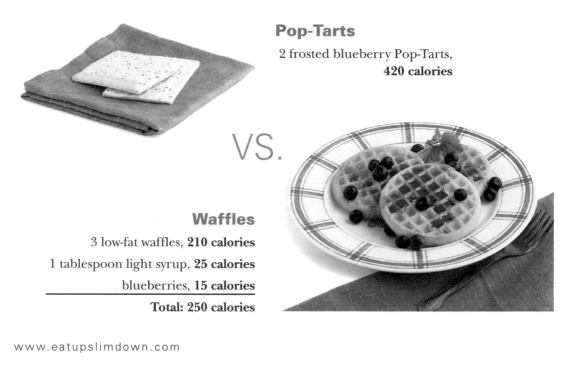

Pop-Tarts
2 frosted blueberry Pop-Tarts,
420 calories

VS.

Waffles
3 low-fat waffles, **210 calories**
1 tablespoon light syrup, **25 calories**
blueberries, **15 calories**
Total: 250 calories

show you how much more food you can have when you eat smart. And those graphic elements are so dramatic, they allow you to keep the comparisons in your mind even after you put the books down, so you can make weight-loss choices forever.

Here's a sample from *Dr. Shapiro's Picture Perfect Weight Loss 30-Day Plan.* All you need to do to get started is make substitutions meal by meal, week by week. Week 1, you'll get bigger, better breakfasts. Week 2, you do lunch. Week 3, what's for dinner gets healthier. And in week 4, you go on a healthy snack attack. At the end of 30 days, you'll feel fuller all day long, but the pounds will keep dropping off— and you will never feel as if you are dieting.

In each of the food-awareness demonstra- tions, the top of the food equation shows a high-calorie food choice. The bottom is a similar but lower-calorie food that will fill you up, satisfy your appetite, and help you shed pounds.

This way of eating works for just about any food-personality type. No matter what your rationale for overeating, you'll have strong visual cues to draw you back on course. You'll know exactly what foods are filling, perfectly acceptable substitutes for the high-fat, high-calorie stuff you've been eating. It can be particularly helpful for the Weekend Eater, who won't have to pay much attention to calories if she sticks with Picture-Perfect choices. It's also a good choice for those in the Baby category, because it minimizes decision making.

GREAT IDEAS FOR WEEK 1

- Think about veggie sausage instead of the meat or poultry versions.
- Try whole grain cereals and breads rather than low-fiber, refined varieties.
- Eat a food you've never had before at three of the week's seven breakfasts.
- Commit to 10 minutes a day of lifestyle exercise, such as walking, gardening, or doing household chores.

Zucchini Bread

1 slice low-fat zucchini bread (6 ounces), **580 calories**

VS.

Fruit and Roll

1 pint strawberries, **80 calories**

1 pound honeydew melon, **80 calories**

1 nectarine, **30 calories**

3 apricots, **60 calories**

¾ pound grapes, **150 calories**

1 pint blackberries, **80 calories**

1 small seeded roll, **100 calories**

Total: 580 calories

Week 2: Lots of Lunch

Lunch is often a quickie meal on the run. But that doesn't mean you can't find a low-calorie, healthy choice at the deli, cafeteria, or sandwich shop—or in your own kitchen.

Roast Beef Sandwich

4 ounces roast beef, **260 calories**

1 kaiser roll, **180 calories**

2 tablespoons sandwich spread, **160 calories**

Total: 600 calories

VS.

Portobello Mushroom Sandwich

1 large portobello mushroom, **30 calories**

1 kaiser roll, **180 calories**

2 tablespoons honey mustard, **30 calories**

Total: 240 calories

Can't give up your favorite fried chicken? Why should you? But think about "flipping the ratio"—filling up on healthy vegetables, so you want less of the high-calorie fried food.

Fried Chicken

2 fried chicken breasts, **800 calories**

VS.

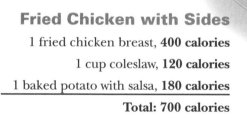

Fried Chicken with Sides

1 fried chicken breast, **400 calories**

1 cup coleslaw, **120 calories**

1 baked potato with salsa, **180 calories**

Total: 700 calories

GREAT IDEAS FOR WEEK 2

Now that you've got some momentum going, pick up the pace.

• Walk briskly for 10 minutes a day.

• Try lunch ideas such as a thick, hearty soup followed by a salad filled with colorful vegetables.

• Hang a sign that says "Honor Thyself" on your refrigerator. Remember, you're not on a diet; you're changing your relationship with food. You're doing this for *you*.

Week 3: Delicious Dinners

For most of us, dinner is the biggest meal of the day. Savor it as you treat yourself to tasty, healthful foods that keep the weight off.

Prime Rib

7 ounces prime rib, **630 calories**

1 stuffed potato with cheese, **350 calories**

1 cup French-cut green beans, **40 calories**

Total: 1,020 calories

VS.

Filet Mignon

7 ounces filet mignon, **480 calories**

1 cup new potatoes with chives, **120 calories**

1 cup French-cut green beans, **40 calories**

Total: 640 calories

Chicken Quesadilla

1 chicken quesadilla, **1,500 calories**

VS.

Shrimp with Salsa

5 ounces shrimp with salsa verde, **150 calories**

1 cup rice and beans, **180 calories**

1 cup baby squash, **40 calories**

Total: 370 calories

GREAT IDEAS FOR WEEK 3

Rev up your weight loss.

- Find an exercise or sport you enjoy enough to do regularly. Do you like dancing? Skiing? Volleyball? Snow-shoeing? Take it up—and keep it up!

- Try an unfamiliar food such as smoked trout, mustard greens, fresh tuna, or lentils.
- Cut down on your time in front of the computer. Get active!

Week 4: Fun Snacks

Sweet? Salty? Sour? What's your pleasure when it comes to snacking? Here are some calorie-saving ideas. Note that while you could eat four boxes of Cracker Jack for the same number of calories as the pretzel, you should stick to just one. That's a mere 120 crunchy, satisfying calories.

Soft Pretzel

1 soft pretzel (6 ounces), **480 calories**

VS.

Cracker Jack

4 boxes Cracker Jack, **480 calories**

Black-and-White Cookie

1 black-and-white mini-cookie (1 ounce), **130 calories**

VS.

Chocolate and Vanilla Frozen Yogurt

2 scoops fat-free frozen yogurt with fresh cherry garnish, **130 calories**

GREAT IDEAS FOR WEEK 4

Keep the pounds coming off now—and beyond—with these can-do approaches.

• Set a regular exercise schedule and make it a priority. Try to work up to 40 minutes of exercise at least every other day.

• Apply the Picture-Perfect Weight-Loss principles when you're eating out. Before you dig into that T-bone steak, for instance, fill up on shrimp cocktail, soup, and a salad. Then choose a smaller cut of beef.

• Continue to incorporate new foods—especially fruits and vegetables—into your diet to keep it fresh and exciting.

● ● ● ● Weight Loss by the Numbers

While controversial, the glycemic index system for rating carbs could be a great way to help you drop pounds.

Invented in the early 1980s by University of Toronto researchers as a tool to help control diabetes, the glycemic index ranks carbohydrate foods by their effect on your blood sugar levels. Today, it's an accepted diet strategy for helping to control diabetes in Canada, Australia, England, and elsewhere. And for that reason alone, it deserves more attention here.

But the biggest surprise of all seems to be that the glycemic index may offer dramatic health benefits not just for diabetics but for almost everyone.

"We're learning that the type of carbs you eat really makes a difference in your health," says glycemic index researcher Christine L. Pelkman, Ph.D., of Pennsylvania State University in State College. And the glycemic index helps you choose the best carbs for you.

You can use the glycemic index to choose meals and snacks that not only help you to shed those stubborn extra pounds but also give you an edge against diabetes, heart attacks, and possibly even cancer.

Good Carbs, Not-So-Good Carbs

The glycemic index (or GI for short) assigns carbohydrate-containing foods a number based on how they affect your blood sugar, or blood glucose, after you eat them. Foods with a GI less than 55 cause only a little blip in blood sugar. Those in the 55 to 70 range raise it a little higher. And carbs with GIs more than 70 send blood sugar soaring. We're learning that low-GI carbs are healthy; high-GI carbs, in excess, are not.

What explains the difference in numbers? No matter what form the carb initially takes—the lactose in milk, the starch in a bagel, the sucrose in table sugar—eventually, your body breaks it down into glucose. Glucose winds up in your bloodstream, fueling your cells. What makes a GI number high or low is how quickly the food breaks down during digestion. The longer your body has to wrestle with the carb to break it down into glucose, the slower the rise in blood glucose and the lower the GI.

But it's not always easy to predict a food's GI. Often, fiber-rich foods have lower GIs. Fiber, especially the soluble type in oats and beans, creates a web in the intestines that traps carb particles. Not surprisingly, beans have low GI numbers.

But when fiber is ground finely as it often is in whole wheat flour, it doesn't present enough of a digestive challenge to lower the GI of the food. That explains why whole wheat bread has a GI number nearly identical to that of white bread. (But whole wheat bread

THE GI MADE EZ

To make the glycemic index work for you, try these practical tips.

1. One per meal. Choose one-third to one-half of your daily starches from the low-GI list (see page 22). You're well on your way if you include one low-GI starch—like a bowl of old-fashioned oatmeal, $\frac{1}{2}$ cup beans, or some lentil soup—per meal.

2. Go whole grain. There are exceptions, but in general, whole grain foods such as barley have a low GI, mainly because their high fiber content slows digestion.

3. Rough it up. The less processed and rougher the grain or flour, the lower the GI. That's why pasta, which is made from a coarse-milled wheat, has a lower GI even if it's not whole grain.

4. Bring it down low. Only have time to make instant rice? Just add some beans. Throwing in a low-GI food brings down the GI rating of the entire meal. Adding some fat or protein also lowers the GI level.

5. Be savvy about snacks. When you snack, you tend to have just one food, all by itself. That's fine if you're having a low-cal snack, whether the GI is high or not. But if you're having a high-GI bagel or doughnut with hundreds of calories, the glucose won't get blunted by other foods. So avoid starchy, high-GI foods as snacks.

6. Load up on fruits, vegetables, and legumes. Most have a low GI, and you'd have to eat pounds of the ones that don't to affect blood sugar. But by the same token, don't binge on low-GI foods that are high in calories, such as candy bars. Gaining weight will raise your blood sugar, too.

7. Reach for the balsamic. GI experts say that the acid in vinegar or lemon juice can substantially blunt the effect of a food on your blood sugar. So adding vinegar to your french fries and making potato salad with a vinaigrette dressing are two smart, tasty ways to lower the GI of potatoes.

is still a healthier choice than white bread because of its extra fiber and other nutrients.)

Surprisingly, table sugar has a lower GI than potatoes have. That's because it's made of two sugars, glucose and fructose. The glucose half sails right into the bloodstream, but the fructose segment has to detour through the liver, where it slowly gets converted into glucose. But the starch molecules in potatoes are strings of glucose. Boiling, baking, or mashing a potato causes the starch molecules to burst, making it so easy for glucose to enter the bloodstream.

High GI = High Risk

The problem with eating lots of high-GI foods is this: When your blood sugar soars, so does the hormone insulin. Insulin's main duty is to scoop up excess blood sugar and store it safely in muscle tissue. In moderation, insulin is a good guy, but it becomes a killer when its levels spike repeatedly, triggering diabetes, heart disease, and possibly cancer.

Unfortunately, insulin is spiking all the time in the millions of Americans who dote on high-GI fare such as bagels, doughnuts, french fries, and other quickly absorbed starchy carbohydrates. Experts point out that modern diets offer vastly more opportunity to eat starchy high-GI foods than the diets on which human beings evolved.

Food-personality types that tend to overeat or binge, such as the Restrained Eater, Slow Gainer, Weekend Eater, or Stress Eater may find they have fewer out-of-control episodes if they pay attention to glycemic index.

Weight-Loss Benefits

The good news is, switching to a low-GI diet results in a minimal outpouring of insulin, and that has healthy ramifications all over your body. As far as weight loss goes, here's what a low-GI diet appears to help you do.

Drop pounds. Ever feel hungry just an hour or two after a meal? It could be because the meal had a high GI. Ironically, high-GI meals cause such a flood of insulin to cope with all the glucose that blood sugar levels wind up lower than if you'd never eaten. And low blood sugar may send out hunger alarms, according to Susan Roberts, Ph.D., professor of nutrition at Tufts University in Boston and author of *Feeding Your Child for Lifelong Health.*

In one study, overweight children (average age 10) at Children's Hospital in Boston spent 4 months on either a low-GI diet or a low-fat diet of equal calories. The

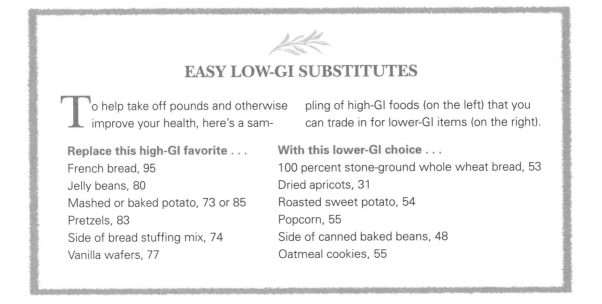

EASY LOW-GI SUBSTITUTES

To help take off pounds and otherwise improve your health, here's a sampling of high-GI foods (on the left) that you can trade in for lower-GI items (on the right).

Replace this high-GI favorite . . .
French bread, 95
Jelly beans, 80
Mashed or baked potato, 73 or 85
Pretzels, 83
Side of bread stuffing mix, 74
Vanilla wafers, 77

With this lower-GI choice . . .
100 percent stone-ground whole wheat bread, 53
Dried apricots, 31
Roasted sweet potato, 54
Popcorn, 55
Side of canned baked beans, 48
Oatmeal cookies, 55

clear winner: the low-GI diet, with an average weight loss of 4.5 pounds compared with 2.8 pounds on the low-fat diet.

Dr. Roberts suspects that high-GI carbs are partly behind America's epidemic levels of obesity. "GI is not the complete answer to everyone's weight problem," she says. "But aside from the research, I am personally convinced that low-GI diets help people lose weight, myself included. My husband and I were eating either a relatively high-GI instant oatmeal or a low-GI Irish oatmeal for breakfast. I'd call and ask how he felt 2 hours later. Both of us noticed a big decrease in hunger with the low-GI oatmeal. Now I've become very aware of the GI of what I eat and quite consistently find myself hungrier after very high GI foods such as bagels, mashed potatoes, and the like."

Stay energetic and alert. Want more stamina? You have greater endurance when you exercise after a low-GI meal compared with a high-GI meal, studies show. And low-GI meals might also give you a mental edge, hints Australian research. People who ate a low-GI breakfast (based on All-Bran) scored higher in a test of alertness than those who ate a high-GI breakfast (based on corn-flakes). "I think the low-GI breakfast increased alertness for two reasons: by fueling the brain with a slow, steady supply of glucose and by staving off hunger. People eating this breakfast didn't get hungry before lunch, while those eating cornflakes did. It's easier to be alert and focused when you're not hungry," speculates

study leader Susanna Holt, R.D., Ph.D., of Sydney University's Human Nutrition Unit.

A Hit Abroad

While organizations in other countries, such as the Canadian Diabetes Association, Australia's International Diabetes Institute, and the World Health Organization, all recommend including low-GI foods as part of managing diabetes, the glycemic index gets only a brief mention in the most recent practice guidelines from the American Diabetes Association (ADA).

"At this point, we don't recommend the glycemic index because not enough is known, and there's no evidence that this method is better than the standard approach of counting carbohydrates," explains Marian Parrot, M.D., vice president of clinical affairs for the ADA. Although Dr. Parrot agrees that the GI is "not harmful" and that "nothing is wrong with the science," her main objection is that it's too complicated—people just can't be expected to remember and deal with all those numbers. And in fact, a substantial group of health experts agree that although the glycemic index may prove useful someday, it is "not ready for prime time."

But in response, Marc Rendell, M.D., director of the Creighton Diabetes Center at Creighton University in Omaha, Nebraska, who wrote an editorial backing the glycemic index in the prestigious *New England Journal of Medicine*, believes there's a bias against publishing research in this area.

"The authorities in the field are too hung up on arithmetic," says Dr. Rendell. "For instance, they bring up the fact that carrots have a high GI, so they're afraid people will

AT-A-GLANCE GLYCEMIC INDEX

Curb your appetite by choosing foods with low GI (glycemic index) numbers. Those with a rating below 55 produce a gradual rise in blood sugar that's easy on the body and keep you satisfied longer. Foods between 55 and 70 are intermediate-GI foods. Foods with high GI numbers (more than 70) make blood sugar as well as insulin levels spike fast. That's not only a health threat but also an invitation to overeat.

The general guideline is to include at least one low-GI food at each meal or snack, advises top GI expert Jennie Brand-Miller, Ph.D., of the University of Sydney in Australia. You don't have to eliminate all high-GI foods, but you can use this guide to work toward more intermediate- and low-GI choices—with the exceptions noted below. So far, there's no fixed rule as to the number of GI points that you are "allowed" at each meal.

Low-Glycemic Index Foods

*Eat sparingly those foods marked with one asterisk. They're high in empty calories.

Less Than 55

Low-fat yogurt, artificially sweetened	14	Apple	36	Long-grain rice	47
Peanuts	14	Pear	36	Parboiled rice	47
Fructose	23	Whole wheat spaghetti	37	Bulgur	48
Plum	24	Tomato soup	38	Canned baked beans	48
Grapefruit	25	Apple juice	41	Grapefruit juice	48
Pearled barley	25	Spaghetti	41	Green peas	48
Peach	28	All-Bran	42	*Chocolate bar	49
Canned peaches, natural juice	30	Canned chickpeas	42	Old-fashioned oatmeal	49
Dried apricots	31	Custard	43	Cheese tortellini	50
Baby lima beans, frozen	32	Grapes	43	*Low-fat ice cream	50
Fat-free milk	32	Orange	43	Canned kidney beans	52
Fettuccine	32	Canned lentil soup	44	Kiwifruit	52
Low-fat yogurt, sugar sweetened	33	Canned pinto beans	45	Banana	53
		Macaroni	45	*Potato chips	54
		Pineapple juice	46	*Pound cake	54
		Banana bread	47	Sweet potato	54

Intermediate-Glycemic Index Foods

*Eat sparingly those foods marked with one asterisk. They're high in empty calories.

55 to 70

Brown rice	55	Bran muffin	60	*Table sugar (sucrose)	65
Canned fruit cocktail	55	Cheese pizza	60	Canned green pea soup	66
Linguine	55	Hamburger bun	61	Instant oatmeal	66
Oatmeal cookies	55	*Ice cream	61	Pineapple	66
Popcorn	55	Beets	64	Angel food cake	67
Sweet corn	55	Canned apricots, light syrup	64	Grape-Nuts	67
White rice	56			Stoned Wheat Thins	67
Orange juice from frozen concentrate	57	Canned black bean soup	64	American rye bread	68
Pita bread	57	Macaroni and cheese	64	Taco shells	68
Canned peaches, heavy syrup	58	Raisins	64	Whole wheat bread	69
		Couscous	65	Life Savers	70
Mini shredded wheats	58	Quick-cooking oatmeal	65	Melba toast	70
Blueberry muffin	59	Rye crispbread	65	White bread	70

High-Glycemic Index Foods

**Don't avoid or even limit high-glycemic index foods marked with two asterisks. They're low in calories and very nutritious.

More Than 70

Golden Grahams	71	Graham crackers	74	Corn Chex	83
Bagel	72	Doughnut	75	Mashed potatoes, instant	83
Corn chips	72	French fries	76	Cornflakes	84
**Watermelon	72	Frozen waffles	76	**Baked potato	85
Honey	73	**Total Cereal	76	Rice Chex	89
Kaiser roll	73	Vanilla wafers	77	Rice, instant	91
Mashed potatoes	73	Grape-Nuts Flakes	80	French bread	95
Bread stuffing mix	74	Jelly beans	80	**Parsnips	97
**Cheerios	74	**Rice cakes	82	Tofu frozen dessert	115
Cream of Wheat, instant	74	Rice Krispies	82		

stop eating carrots." But GI experts never advise avoiding high-GI foods that are low-calorie vegetables or fruits. "If high-GI foods such as carrots are also low in calories, you'd have to eat pounds of them to make much of an impact on blood sugar," says Thomas Wolever, M.D., of the University of Toronto and coauthor of *The Glucose Revolution.*

Dr. Wolever recommends targeting those high-GI foods that are also high in calories, such as baked goods, highly refined breakfast cereals, and potatoes. Start to replace them with lower-GI foods, such as trading in bagels for 100 percent stone-ground whole wheat bread, instant rice for barley, or cornflakes in favor of All-Bran. "Switching to these low-GI starches," says Dr. Wolever, "can make a tremendous difference in your health."

Be a Square

Eating minimeals but gaining weight? Here's why you may want to stop "grazing" and rediscover three hearty meals a day.

You've no doubt heard of "grazing"—eating four to six small meals a day instead of the traditional three—as a way to lose those unwanted pounds. Some research suggests that this eating pattern of snacking between meals or eating minimeals throughout the day may help keep insulin levels under control, lower cholesterol, prevent heartburn, and, yes, even help you lose weight.

It's still good advice for many people. Ostrich or Restrained Eater food personality types may find that this way of eating works well for them. And Stress Eaters may find that it gives them a structure that excludes

WHEN SNACKING IS ESSENTIAL

Here are a few situations when a snack may be necessary.

• You're going to work out, and you haven't eaten in 3 or more hours.
• Your next meal is 5 to 6 hours away (unless that meal is breakfast).
• You didn't eat enough, and you're feeling real, physiological hunger between meals.

When you do snack, choose healthful and light foods, such as an egg-white omelet, a cup of soup, some yogurt, or a banana.

"zoned out" eating. But for others, it can lead to calorie disaster and unwanted pounds, according to some weight-loss experts. Here's how to find out if your eating pattern is making you fat and how to change it so you'll drop pounds without feeling deprived.

Is Grazing Making You Fat?

The bottom line for weight loss is that you have to burn more calories than you consume. For some people, snacking between meals curbs their appetite so they eat fewer calories overall. But for others, it can substantially increase the amount of calories they eat and lead to weight gain.

Snacking makes you fat when "snacking begets snacking," says Stephen Gullo, Ph.D., author of *Thin Tastes Better.* The old potato chip ad "Betcha can't eat just one" hit the nail on the head. Certain combinations of salt, sugar, and crunch can make it virtually impossible to stop at one or two bites. "One potato chip can lead to 1,000 calories," Dr. Gullo says.

That's what gets lots of us in trouble. If you're not satisfied with just one cookie, you might find it much easier if you don't start eating them.

And it's not just a taste thing. Snack foods can stimulate the appetite by their effects on our blood sugar, Dr. Gullo explains. Most snack foods are made with white flour, sugar, and very little fiber, even ones such as pretzels that we think of as healthy because they're low in fat. That combination of ingredients is just the thing to send blood sugar soaring and crashing, leaving hunger and the hunt for the next snack in its wake.

Most of the time, our bodies don't physiologically need the calories. Instead, we're snacking out of habit, boredom, loneliness, or stress. A survey of more than 1,000 adults revealed that nearly one-third of women snack purely out of boredom.

Rediscover "Hunger"

When you snack all day, you never let yourself get hungry. And eating out of hunger is critical to successful weight loss, says Marlene Lesson, R.D., nutrition director at Structure House, a Durham, North Carolina, residential treatment center for weight control.

Hunger usually means your body actually needs the calories. But if you never feel hungry, you never learn to recognize your body's cues that it's really time to eat: You've burned off the calories from the previous meal, and it's time to stoke up your engine again. Eating three well-spaced-out meals a day will reconnect you to those all-important hunger signals.

"Since I stopped snacking, I go into my meals a little hungry and really enjoy them," says 40-something Lissa Goldberg, a Manhattan mother of four who lost 40 pounds in a year. Her hunger signals were weak or nonexistent on her previous pattern: lunch and dinner but no breakfast plus afternoon-through-evening snacking.

Eating when you're not truly hungry can make you fat, according to one French study published in the *American Journal of Clinical Nutrition*, in which subjects ate a lunch

SNACKS VS. SQUARES: HOW THEY STACK UP

Minimeals, or snacks, can actually add up to more calories. Check out this side-by-side comparison with three squares a day, and see how you can enjoy heartier meals for fewer calories, and still lose weight without feeling hungry.

The Snacks

8:30 A.M. (breakfast)
Coffee with fat-free milk and sugar

10:00 A.M.
Fat-free muffin and coffee with fat-free milk and sugar

1:00 P.M. (lunch)
Bagel with fat-free cream cheese and fruit salad

2:30 P.M.
Bag of pretzels and bottle of sweetened iced tea

4:00 P.M.
Fat-free fruit yogurt

7:00 P.M. (dinner)
Salad with fat-free Italian dressing

8:00 P.M.
Pint of fat-free frozen yogurt

10:30 P.M.
20 wheat crackers

The Squares

8:00 A.M. (breakfast)
½ cup high-fiber bran cereal with ½ cup blueberries and 1 cup fat-free milk
Slice whole wheat toast with 2 teaspoons peanut butter
Coffee with fat-free milk and sugar

12:30 P.M. (lunch)
1 cup turkey-and-bean chili topped with 2 tablespoons low-fat grated Cheddar
¾ cup brown rice
1 cup steamed broccoli drizzled with ½ teaspoon olive oil and a spritz of lemon juice
Glass fat-free milk
1⅓ cups fruit salad

5:30 P.M. (dinner)
Spinach and feta omelet (1 egg, 2 egg whites, ¾ cup steamed spinach, 3 tablespoons crumbled feta cheese cooked in 2 teaspoons margarine or oil)
Slice whole wheat bread
½ cup low-fat frozen yogurt topped with ½ banana and 1 teaspoon chocolate syrup

1,926 calories, 21 grams fat (10 percent of total calories), 15 grams fiber

1,500 calories, 42 grams fat (25 percent of total calories), 35 grams fiber

that left them full, then followed it up with a snack. When researchers did blood tests, they found that snacking when you're not hungry puts your body in a fat-storage mode; instead of using the calories, it saves them for later. And the subjects who had that snack "chaser" didn't compensate by eating less at dinner.

The Three-Squares Eating Plan

Here's how to go from the "nonstop buffet" to three meals a day without feeling ravenous.

Make a plan. Write down meals for the next few days or the upcoming week.

Eat filling meals. "My hardest job is getting clients to eat enough at a meal. When they don't, they're looking for a snack shortly afterward," says Lesson. (See "Snacks vs. Squares: How They Stack Up" for appropriate meal sizes.)

"When I was snacking, my meals often consisted of plain, steamed veggies and a little pasta with tomato sauce—no lasagna, no creamed corn, no chicken salad, nothing more filling, and never dessert. I ate that way to make up for all the calories I was getting

from my snacks," says one former grazer. "But then I'd come away from meals not really satisfied. So I was setting myself up to snack again."

Don't miss meals. Cutting down to only two meals a day won't make you any slimmer. Your body knows how many calories it needs, and when you skip a meal, your body demands those calories later—often when you're too tired to prepare a meal and junk food looks appealing.

Find a balance. "Make sure your meals contain protein, carbohydrates, and a little fat," says Robin Kanarek, Ph.D., professor of nutrition at Tufts University in Boston. A tablespoon of peanut butter on your morning toast, tuna in your salad, or stir-fried vegetables instead of steamed help you feel fuller longer. Balancing even snacks this way reduces the glycemic index of foods, too, slowing absorption.

Don't forget roughage. "Fiber is nature's appetite suppressant," says Dr. Gullo. Studies show that fiber keeps you feeling satisfied on fewer calories and helps keep blood sugar on an even keel, which staves off hunger. For breakfast, that means 100 per-

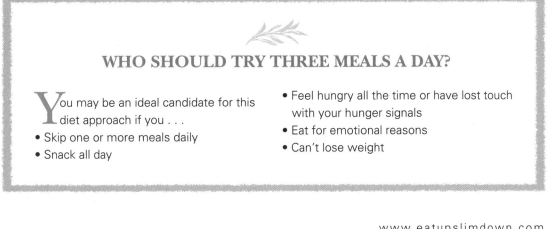

WHO SHOULD TRY THREE MEALS A DAY?

You may be an ideal candidate for this diet approach if you . . .
- Skip one or more meals daily
- Snack all day

- Feel hungry all the time or have lost touch with your hunger signals
- Eat for emotional reasons
- Can't lose weight

cent whole grain breads and waffles and bran cereals. The rest of the day, make it a point to eat more 100 percent whole grain breads, whole wheat pasta, barley, beans, fruits, and vegetables.

Keep a journal. "Keeping a food diary made me conscious of everything I ate and helped me stop snacking," says Goldberg. "I was so unaware of what I was eating." For instance, she wasn't counting the daily 15 cups of decaf, half-filled with whole milk, which racked up more than 1,000 calories. Those in the Ostrich and Baby categories, especially, can see the truth of their eating habits if they can keep a food diary for three days or so.

Make it simple. Preparing dinner may seem overwhelming if you haven't done it in a while or need to whip something together after work. Use prewashed greens, precut vegetables and fruits, prepared chicken, canned beans, scrambled eggs, and other easy foods. For the super busy, Lesson suggests supermarket shopping online or by phone with home delivery. Or have someone cook for you: The American Personal Chef Association can match you up with a cook who will deliver a week's worth of meals for a reasonable price. (Call 800-644-8389 or visit www.personalchef.com.)

Purge the pantry. "Get the right foods in the house and the wrong ones out," says Dr. Gullo. This includes deep-sixing low-fat cookies and crackers—even health-food-store versions, which are still loaded with calories. Worried about your kids' snack attacks? Hey, what's sweeter than a banana or a peach? "Kids can get all the junk they want when they're away from home, so there's no need

to have it in the house," Lesson says. You're not depriving your kids; in fact, you're helping them grow up with healthy eating habits. Weekend Eaters can especially benefit from this strategy.

Address emotional eating. Here's Goldberg's quick-fix solution: "I take a walk when I get the urge to snack, and when I get home, I'm okay." But distraction—making a phone call, reading a magazine, planning your week—is often not enough; you may also have to work on changing the stress, loneliness, or other issues that trigger snacking.

Be happy with your choices. When you sit down to breakfast, lunch, or dinner, choose foods you really love. Have that lasagna or meat loaf and gravy or a grilled cheese sandwich. Just take reasonable portions and fill the rest of your plate with lots of veggies. Knowing you can look forward to a fun meal keeps you from feeling deprived when you pass up snacks. This strategy can suit Baby and Good/Bad Fairy Eaters.

Feel the power. As with any other area of your life, getting organized and creating structure—this time with your eating habits—give you a sense of control, self-mastery, and empowerment. "I'm now much more focused in so many areas of my life," says Goldberg. "Three meals a day makes eating foolproof. Even if I fall off the wagon, I'm relaxed, because I have a structure to go back to."

It's a no-brainer. The bottom line is simplicity: You eat your food in three meals a day, period. Between meals is a no-food zone. You end up spending less time thinking about food and more time feeling satisfied.

Turn On Your Weight-Loss Hormones!

Raging hormones can sabotage almost any weight-loss strategy. But evidence suggests that taking advantage of natural mechanisms in your body may help you manage your weight, shape, and appetite.

Whether it's their period, menopause, stress, a hysterectomy, or plain old heredity, women have felt vulnerable to hormonal cravings and sluggish metabolism for years, with little to prove it but instinct. Now science is uncovering several bona fide links between women's hormones, hunger, and fat metabolism.

What follows is a hormone-harmonizing plan that may be worth trying if you've had trouble trimming down in the past. In each of 8 weeks, you'll learn new ways to keep the levels of "snacking" hormones from inching up into the danger zone or to encourage the levels of "feel-good" hormones to rise. It's a program designed to help you live life in balance and stick with your commitment to healthy eating.

Soothe Your Stress

WEEK 1

If you're like many people, you've got a demanding job, a family that needs you, and a never-ending to-do list. No wonder you feel tired or depressed, anxious or irritable. Or perhaps you can't sleep (although you have no problem eating).

29

Sex—or at least good sex—may be a distant memory.

All these are hallmark symptoms of chronic stress—the cumulative load of minor, everyday annoyances or frustrations that are all too commonplace.

Unrelenting stress can launch the female body into major hormonal action. The chemical and electrical dance among the brain, various glands, and the sympathetic nervous system activates the fight-or-flight response, the body's involuntary response to a threat that makes our hearts pound and our breaths shorten. Chief among the hormones released during this response is the stress hormone cortisol.

Cortisol automatically kicks up your appetite, prompting you to want not only huge quantities of food but especially sweets and simple carbohydrates. These are foods that make insulin levels spike and then plummet, which may leave you feeling hungrier than ever and eating again, says Pamela M. Peeke, M.P.H., M.D., assistant clinical professor of medicine at the University of Maryland School of Medicine in Baltimore and author of *Fight Fat after Forty.*

Cortisol also contributes to the deposition of "stress fat," which is concentrated in the last place in your body you need it: deep in your tummy. Stress fat doesn't just make your waistband tight. It's also associated with high cholesterol, high blood pressure, and type 2 diabetes—the things that cause heart disease.

To help reset your internal stress-o-meter to normal levels, and perhaps reduce stress-related hormonal cravings, experts recommend the following strategies.

Talk "calming sense" into yourself.
Try silently repeating a soothing word or phrase to yourself, such as "peace" or "This, too, shall pass," while taking slow, deep breaths through your nose. It's the truth, and it can steer you away from emotional eating, which isn't going to help things anyway.

Put photos in your "stress zones."
Choose shots that transport you back to a perfect moment in your life. Clip a photo from your anniversary trip to Hawaii to your car's visor to calm you when you're stuck in traffic. Place beautifully framed pictures of your children in your work area. When stress closes in, turn to those images. Recall in vivid detail what you saw, heard, smelled, and felt in those moments. Change the photos often to stimulate soothing memories.

Schedule regular play periods.
Whether it's assembling a 1,000-piece jigsaw puzzle or going sledding with the kids, play of any kind distracts us from our worries, providing us with a temporary refuge from everyday stress. Aim for 15 minutes a day. The word *silly* derives from the Greek *selig* meaning "blessed." There is something sacred in being able to be silly. We forget ourselves and become free.

Learn a relaxation technique. Not everyone can automatically relax, and the harder they try, the more "un-laxed" they get. If you're one of them, find a teacher. Many yoga teachers teach progressive relaxation. So do some hypnotherapists or biofeedback instructors. And both transcendental meditation and mindfulness meditation (available as courses) can teach you to relax. Or you can try the Relaxation Response popularized by Herbert Benson, M.D., in his book *The Relaxation Response.* It's been shown to reduce blood levels of stress hormones and to reduce high blood pressure.

Laugh, Especially at Yourself
WEEK 2

For more than 20 years, Lee S. Berk, M.P.H., Dr.P.H., has studied the effect of mirthful laughter and humor on our hormones and immune system. But his findings are anything but silly.

"If we put what we currently understand about laughter's effects on the neuroendocrine and immune systems into a pill, it would require FDA approval," says Dr. Berk, associate research professor at the Loma Linda University School of Medicine and Public Health in California. Dr. Berk's research has found that laughter causes significant drops in our levels of stress hormones.

In one study, Dr. Berk and colleagues had six people watch an hour-long humor video, which they chose themselves. Blood tests showed that the video watchers had 30 percent less cortisol in their blood and significantly lower levels of another stress hormone, epinephrine, during and after the tape compared with a group that sat quietly.

Kids laugh about 400 times a day; grownups, about 15. Our suggestions here can help strengthen your humor "muscles," says Paul McGhee, Ph.D., president of The Laughter Remedy in Wilmington, Delaware.

Laugh at yourself. "Laughter is like mercy; it heals. When you can laugh at yourself, you are free," says Ted Loder, author of *My Heart Is in My Mouth.* Being able to short-circuit self-pity or loathing with a good laugh at yourself may help you out of a spot if you're an emotional eater and getting ready to chow down.

Keep alert for inadvertently funny headlines or ads. One of Dr. McGhee's favorites, posted in a restaurant in Mexico City: "The water served here has been personally passed by the manager."

Take a 5-minute laugh break every day. Keep a collection of jokes or pictures that always set you off. Cultivate friendships with people who can make you laugh.

Lighten up your commute. Alternate your favorite tunes with a cassette or CD of your favorite comedian or a humorous book on tape.

At the video store, head toward the comedy section. Sample everything, from reruns of *I Love Lucy* episodes to movies such as *Shrek* or *Dr. Doolittle 2.* And don't forget classic performances by comics such as Steve Martin, Gilda Radner, Bill Cosby, Lily Tomlin, Lenny Bruce, or John Belushi.

Treat Yourself to Massage
WEEK 3

Regular rubdowns aren't frivolous indulgences—they can benefit your hormones in measurable ways. Deep-pressure massage reduces blood levels of norepinephrine, epinephrine, and cortisol, the same hormone that stimulates appetite and helps pile on deep abdominal fat. At the same time, massage stimulates nerves that cause heart rate

PREVENT PMS MUNCHIES

If out-of-control cravings drive you to the cookie jar every month, here's what you can do to avoid packing on extra pounds over the long haul.

First, realize that it's normal to experience food cravings around the time of your period, says Pamela M. Peeke, M.P.H., M.D., assistant clinical professor of medicine at the University of Maryland School of Medicine in Baltimore and author of *Fight Fat after Forty*.

The menstrual cycle delivers a double whammy of two different hormone groups increasing at the same time: sex hormones (estrogen and progesterone) and stress hormones (cortisol and epinephrine). Some say that the neurotransmitter serotonin also fluctuates with your monthly cycle. These changes drive up your appetite and prompt you to eat the kind of foods that increase your insulin levels.

To minimize the munchies, here's what Dr. Peeke recommends.

- Eat a little more protein, such as an egg or a cup of beans, at every meal when you have PMS to help prevent wild cravings. "Protein can give you an exquisite sense of satisfaction," says Dr. Peeke.
- Get your calcium (the recommended Daily Value of 1,000 milligrams a day from food and supplements). Research shows that it works to reduce PMS cravings.
- Exercise, no matter how bad you feel. The aerobic charge will dampen your appetite.

and breathing to slow down. It also brightens mood and reduces perception of pain. That's because it causes a rise in levels of two mood-regulating brain chemicals, serotonin and dopamine. All this is good news if you're a stress eater. When you know your week is going to be hectic, schedule a massage instead of a pig-out. Or do self-massage.

Tame tension in 10 minutes or less. Give yourself a head and scalp massage. Start at the nape of your neck, and work your fingers in a circular motion around your scalp, until you've covered every inch. Massage between your eyebrows, moving up along your forehead, then down to your temples. Massage your cheeks, chin, jaw, nose, and around your mouth. Return to your forehead and massage along your eyebrows and below your eyes.

Try partner massage. Research shows that people who give a massage also reduce stress hormone levels. Use pressure deep enough so that the area being massaged turns slightly whiter. Choose soothing, sensual surroundings, in a warm room on a firm, comfortable surface such as a futon or mat. Use a light oil that does not dry up with air contact (almond oil is great). Try adding a few drops of essential oil of lavender to promote relaxation. You can find essential herbs in health food stores.

Catch Some Quality Zzzs

WEEK 4

Besides making you cranky, sleep loss (getting less than 8 hours of sleep a night) may contribute to weight gain by dramatically disrupting the hormones that control your eating habits and your metabolism.

In one small study, researchers in the University of Chicago's department of medicine compared the hormone levels of 11 men while they got 8 hours of sleep for several nights, followed by several nights of a mere 4 hours in bed. During the sleep-debt stage, the men's ability to process glucose was impaired as much as that of a person with type 2 diabetes—indicating that sleep debt could lead to insulin resistance, a condition some experts think encourages obesity.

In all the afternoons that followed a sleep-deprived night, the men also had consistently elevated levels of cortisol, which encourages cells to store more fat, particularly when paired with insulin resistance. Not to mention that levels of thyroid hormone, the metabolism powerhouse, were lowered during sleep deprivation.

Whether you have trouble falling asleep or staying asleep, these expert tips should help.

Get outside. The release of hormones in your brain is regulated by the nerve impulses sent by your retinas in response to light. In other words, living by the earth's natural cycle of light and darkness keeps your serotonin and cortisol at their proper levels. Getting at least 30 minutes of natural light a day helps reset our inner alarm clocks, so we'll want to fall asleep at the right time, says Joyce Walsleben, Ph.D., director of the Sleep Disorders Center at New York University in New York City and author of *A Woman's Guide to Sleep: Guaranteed Solutions for a Good Night's Rest.*

Take a walk. In one study of more than 700 people, those who took daily walks were one-third less likely to have trouble sleeping until their normal wake-up time. Those who walked briskly slashed the risk of any sleep disorder by half. Regular exercise alleviates stress and also raises body temperature, which primes us for slumber.

Reduce or eliminate stimulants, such as caffeinated coffee, tea, soda, chocolate, and nicotine, before going to bed. Also, avoid alcohol, which is sedating but disrupts sleep.

Make your bedroom dark. Darkness stimulates the production of melatonin, a light-sensitive hormone produced by the pineal gland, which is located in the brain. Some evidence suggests that supplementing with this hormone can help remedy insomnia. (Take only temporarily under the supervision of a knowledgeable medical doctor.) To manipulate this hormone naturally, invest in thick, heavy curtains or don an eye mask.

Make Love—It's Good for You

WEEK 5

The connection between sex and your waistline isn't as far-fetched as you might think. The more we do "it," the more endorphins our brains release. These "neurohormones"—chemicals released in the brain during exercise and after orgasm—are natural painkillers and help to alleviate anxiety, generate contentment, and promote deep, restful sleep. All three of those things can lead to a calmer lifestyle and less stressed-out eating. Don't reach for your plate when what you really need and want is your mate. Here are some warm-up suggestions.

Pay attention to subtle sexual cues. When you feel the slightest pulse of desire, follow through on it. See if you can detect any cycles of desire. Are you more receptive at a certain time of day or in a particular place? Take advantage of it.

Make time for sex. If sexual desire doesn't come to you spontaneously, you might still enjoy sex once you're aroused. But if you aren't highly motivated, you may have to deliberately schedule time for lovemaking. Make "dates" and keep them.

Eat Right

WEEK 6

A healthy diet can have a dramatically positive effect on hormone levels, and in turn, help balance your appetite, energy level, and fat-to-muscle ratio. The basic plan is a diet loaded with whole grains, fresh fruits and vegetables, and low-fat or fat-free dairy products, with less red meat and processed foods.

A high-fiber diet can help keep your blood sugar levels stable. Otherwise, foods made with refined grains, such as white bread, white pasta, and white rice, are digested quickly and speeded into the bloodstream as the body's primary source of fuel: blood sugar. This rapid breakdown triggers a flood of insulin, the hormone that ferries the sugar into the cells.

Shortly thereafter, blood sugar levels drop precipitously, which signals the adrenal glands to release more cortisol. By contrast, beans, brown rice, and whole grain cereals take much longer to digest. Thus, insulin levels rise gradually, blood sugar levels remain steady, and cortisol levels don't skyrocket.

Here are some other diet tips to help trick your weight-control hormones with food.

Make breakfast a must. It is the "single greatest factor in maintaining portion control and stable hormone levels throughout the day," says Geoffrey Redmond, M.D., director of the Hormone Center of New York in New York City and author of *The Good News about Women's Hormones.*

Have a protein appetizer 10 minutes

A BOWL OF WEIGHT LOSS

Your key to weight loss may be hiding in your cereal bowl. People who regularly enjoy ready-to-eat breakfast cereal with fruit weigh less than those who skip breakfast, according to research.

Cereal eaters also eat less fat and cholesterol and more fiber during the day. "Cereal creates a healthy start to your day. It's nutritious and low-fuss; plus, cereal eaters are likely to make smart choices at other meals," says study author Gladys Block, Ph.D., director of the public health nutrition program at the University of California, Berkeley.

Choose a fiber-rich cereal and make it more appealing by adding fresh fruit or a sprinkling of nuts. Some choices you may want to try:

General Mills Multi-Bran Chex (1 cup), 200 calories, 8 grams fiber

Kashi Seven Whole Grains & Sesame (¾ cup), 90 calories, 8 grams fiber

Post Cinna-Cluster Raisin Bran (1 cup), 220 calories, 7 grams fiber

Kellogg's Honey Frosted Mini-Wheats (24 biscuits), 200 calories, 6 grams fiber

Post Fruit & Fiber (1 cup), 190 calories, 6 grams fiber

---

before each meal. It's possible that doing this sends your body the right signals not to overeat, since protein stimulates the production of the appetite-regulating hormones cholecystokinin and glucagon. Have string cheese or a very small handful of nuts before you sit down to dine.

Consume three to four servings of high-calcium foods. One serving equals 1 cup of fat-free or 1 percent milk, 1 cup of fat-free or low-fat yogurt, 1 ounce of reduced-fat cheese, or 1 cup of calcium-fortified cereal, orange juice, or soy milk. One study showed that people who got three to four servings of low-fat dairy products a day lost 70 percent more weight and 64 percent more fat than people eating the same number of calories minus the calcium. Researchers think that when your body doesn't get enough calcium, it triggers fat cells to store fat and get bigger.

Substitute soy. Replacing animal products such as whole milk, hamburger, sausages, bacon, ground beef, chicken, or even spare ribs with any one of the delicious soy substitutes now on the market reduces the amount of unhealthy saturated fat you consume. Plus, it provides soy protein, which helps to reduce LDL cholesterol.

Use Herbs to Destress

WEEK 7

Herbs called adaptogens help our bodies adapt to various physical stresses such as infections, sleep deprivation, and extreme altitudes, as well as fortify us from the physical effects of emotional stress. Adaptogens help the body achieve balance, or homeostasis. They help it maintain or regain equilibrium in the face of a changing outside environment. That's good because it means you recover from stress faster, so you're less likely to indulge in stress overeating. Use these herbs to get through a period of intense, unremitting stress, not every day. Look for herbs in health food stores.

Note: Check with your doctor before you begin using herbs.

Licorice. One of its constituents, glycyrrhizin, is structurally similar to cortisol, and herbal healers often prescribe licorice to strengthen the adrenal glands. Dried root: two 500-milligram tablets three times a day. Tincture: 1:1 strength: 20 drops, twice a day; 1:5 strength: 1 teaspoon, twice a day. (Do not use if you have diabetes, high blood pressure, liver or kidney disorders, or low potassium levels. Overuse can lead to fluid retention and high blood pressure. Do not take for longer than 4 to 6 weeks. Not recommended during pregnancy.)

Siberian ginseng. This herb appears to reduce the response of the adrenal cortex,

the part of the adrenals that pump out cortisol. Dried root: two 500-milligram tablets three times a day. Tincture: 1:1 strength: 20 drops, three times a day; 1:5 strength: 1 teaspoon, three times a day.

Astragalus. Both ancient Chinese healers and modern-day healers have used the root of this herb to counteract the debilitating effect of stress on the immune system. Dried root: two 500-milligram tablets three times a day. Tincture: 1:1 strength: 20 drops, three times a day; 1:5 strength: 1 teaspoon, three times a day.

Move That Body

WEEK 8

Lacing up your sneakers is virtually a call to action for the hormones that reverse fat storage and curb eating. "Your muscles are loaded with insulin receptors," says Christiane Northrup, M.D., author of *Women's Bodies, Women's Wisdom* and *The Wisdom of Menopause.* "The more muscle mass you have and the more heat you generate from your muscles on a regular basis, the more efficiently you'll use insulin and burn carbohydrates and body fat."

There's strong evidence that moderate exercise—like a brisk walk or a 45-minute date with the Nautilus machines—also triggers the release of "pleasure chemicals" known as endorphins. Finally, working up a good sweat activates the "feel-good" neurotransmitters dopamine and serotonin, which reduce the symptoms of depression.

Here's a basic exercise plan.

Note: Before you begin any exercise program, talk with your doctor.

Get your heart pumping. Try for 30 minutes of moderate activity, such as brisk walking or bicycling, at least five times a week for fitness. Or 45 to 60 minutes of moderate activity at least five times a week for weight loss.

Lift weights. Muscles are your calorie-burning furnace, so the better you maintain them, the higher you keep your metabolic rate. "Weight training is essential for women over 40 to help compensate for the decreased muscle mass from falling hormones," explains Dr. Peeke.

Find your passion. Choose activities that fit your temperament and body type. Do you feel more comfortable exercising in a group or by yourself? Do you dislike routine, or do you thrive on it? Do you like to be outdoors or do you prefer air-conditioned comfort? Can your knees and back handle the pounding of a run?

Get back in the saddle. Don't allow one missed workout to derail your fitness program. Missing one workout—or even several—doesn't undo all the good you've done. If you're working out three times a week, you'll still be okay if you miss no more than two to four times in a month.

Desserts

Chocolate Chippers

75 Calories

2¼ cups unbleached all-purpose flour
¼ cup cornstarch
1 teaspoon baking soda
½ teaspoon salt
¼ cup butter or margarine, softened
2 ounces reduced-fat cream cheese, softened
¾ cup sugar
¾ cup packed light brown sugar
1 egg
1 egg white
1 teaspoon vanilla extract
¾ cup chocolate chips

Preheat the oven to 375°F. Coat a baking sheet with cooking spray.

In a medium bowl, combine the flour, cornstarch, baking soda, and salt. In a large bowl, combine the butter or margarine and cream cheese. With an electric mixer on medium speed, beat for 1 minute, or until smooth. Add the granulated sugar and brown sugar and beat until light and creamy. Add the egg, egg white, and vanilla extract and beat until smooth. Reduce the mixer speed to low. Add the flour mixture in 2 additions, beating just until combined. With a spoon, stir in the chocolate chips.

Drop the dough by rounded teaspoonfuls onto the prepared baking sheet. Bake for 9 to 12 minutes, or until golden. Remove the cookies to a rack to cool. Repeat to bake all the cookies.

Makes 40 cookies

Per cookie: *75 calories, 1 g protein, 12 g carbohydrates, 2 g fat, 10 mg cholesterol, 85 mg sodium, 0 g dietary fiber*

Diet Exchanges: *0 milk, 0 vegetable, 0 fruit, 1 bread, 0 meat, ½ fat*

Oat Bran Cookies

—Robin James, Broken Arrow, Oklahoma

"This recipe will handle your taste for sweets and provide your body with plenty of healthy fiber."

¼ cup butter or margarine, softened
¾ cup packed brown sugar
2 egg whites or ½ cup liquid egg substitute
½ teaspoon vanilla extract
¾ cup unbleached all-purpose flour
¼ teaspoon baking soda
1 cup oat bran

Preheat the oven to 350°F. Coat a baking sheet with cooking spray.

In a medium bowl, with an electric mixer on medium speed, beat the butter and sugar until creamed. Add the egg whites or egg substitute and vanilla extract and mix well. Stir in the flour and baking soda until well-combined. Stir in the oat bran. Drop the dough by level tablespoons onto the prepared baking sheet.

Bake for 10 minutes, or until golden brown. Let stand for 1 minute before removing from the baking sheet. Remove the cookies to a rack to cool.

Makes 24 cookies

Per cookie: *74 calories, 2 g protein, 13 g carbohydrates, 2 g fat, 6 mg cholesterol, 44 mg sodium, 1 g dietary fiber*

Diet Exchanges: *0 milk, 0 vegetable, 0 fruit, 1 bread, 0 meat, ½ fat*

SECRETS OF WEIGHT-LOSS WINNERS

• After I bake a cake, I poke a few holes in the top and pour a glass of fruit juice over it. Tastes great, stays moist, and does not need any frosting.

—Sheela Shankar, Woodbridge, New Jersey

• If you must have chocolate, buy the small candy bar sizes and freeze all but one.

—Judy Lanyon, Bald Knob, Arkansas

Lemon Mini Tarts

—Janine Brennan, Brighton, Michigan

" These tarts are great for sugar lovers. Each one packs a big, satisfying lemony punch! "

TARTS

3 packages frozen mini phyllo tart shells (45 shells), thawed

1 cup sugar

⅓ cup cornstarch

1½ cups water

¾ cup liquid egg substitute

3 tablespoons light butter

½ cup lemon juice

2 teaspoons grated lemon peel

2 drops yellow food coloring

MERINGUE

2 egg whites

¼ teaspoon vanilla extract

⅛ teaspoon cream of tartar

2 tablespoons sugar

To make the tarts:

Preheat the oven to 400°F. Coat 2 or 3 baking sheets with cooking spray. Place the tart shells on the prepared baking sheets.

Combine the sugar and cornstarch in a medium saucepan over medium heat. Gradually add the water and cook, stirring constantly, for 1 minute, or until the mixture thickens and begins to boil. Boil and stir for 1 minute.

Place the egg substitute in a large bowl. Stir in half the sugar mixture and add back to the saucepan. Bring to a boil and stir for 1 minute. Remove from the heat and stir in the butter, lemon juice, lemon peel, and food coloring. Evenly divide the mixture among the tart shells.

To make the meringue:

In a large clean bowl, with an electric mixer on medium speed, beat the egg whites until foamy. Add the vanilla extract and cream of tartar and beat until soft peaks form. Beat in the sugar, 1 tablespoon at a time, until stiff, glossy peaks form.

Spoon the meringue into the tarts, carefully spreading to the edges to prevent shrinking.

Bake for 5 minutes, or until golden. Cool on a rack.

Makes 45 tarts

Per tart: *70 calories, 2 g protein, 13 g carbohydrates, 1 g fat, 0 mg cholesterol, 75 mg sodium, 0 g dietary fiber*

Diet Exchanges: *0 milk, 0 vegetable, 0 fruit, 1 bread, 0 meat, 0 fat*

Gold Rush Lemon Bars

98 Calories

CRUST

2 cups unbleached all-purpose flour

⅔ cup confectioners' sugar

½ cup butter or margarine, cut into small pieces

FILLING

3 lemons

1½ cups sugar

¼ cup unbleached all-purpose flour

1 cup liquid egg substitute

2 tablespoons confectioners' sugar

To make the crust:

Preheat the oven to 350°F. Coat a jelly-roll pan with cooking spray.

In a medium bowl, combine the flour and confectioners' sugar. Cut in the margarine or butter until the mixture resembles coarse meal. Press evenly into the bottom of the prepared pan. Bake for 10 minutes, or until lightly browned. Cool on a rack.

To make the filling:

Grate the rind from 2 of the lemons into a medium bowl. Cut all the lemons in half and squeeze the juice into the bowl. Discard the lemons. Whisk in the sugar, flour, and egg substitute until smooth. Pour over the prepared crust. Bake for 18 minutes, or until the filling is set when lightly touched in the center and the edges are beginning to color. Cool on a rack. When completely cooled, sift the confectioners' sugar over the top.

Makes 36 bars

Per bar: *98 calories, 2 g protein, 17 g carbohydrates, 3 g fat, 5 mg cholesterol, 10 mg sodium, 0 g dietary fiber*

Diet Exchanges: *0 milk, 0 vegetable, 0 fruit, 1 bread, 0 meat, ½ fat*

Kitchen Tip

Lemon bars are best served within 48 hours of baking. For an interesting variation, replace the lemons with limes or oranges. Or use a combination of these citrus fruits for a tropical taste.

SECRETS OF WEIGHT-LOSS WINNERS

• I substitute applesauce for oil in recipes. Baked goods are moister, and it even works in bread machines.

—**Donna Vomachka, Springfield, Illinois**

• I've found that replacing white flour with whole wheat in baked goods makes me feel full while eating less.

—**Sheela Shankar, Woodbridge, New Jersey**

• Soy milk is a thick, rich-tasting addition to pudding, cereal, oatmeal, and shakes, without the fat that cream has. Try the flavored varieties like vanilla, chocolate, mocha, and hazelnut for a real treat.

—**Amy Stroud, Campbell, Texas**

Walnut Brownies

116 Calories

1 cup unbleached all-purpose flour

¾ cup unsweetened cocoa powder

½ teaspoon baking powder

¼ teaspoon salt

¼ cup butter or margarine, softened

2 ounces reduced-fat cream cheese, softened

1½ cups sugar

1 egg

2 egg whites

1 tablespoon vanilla extract

½ cup coarsely chopped walnuts

Preheat the oven to 350°F. Coat a 13" × 9" baking pan with cooking spray.

In a medium bowl, combine the flour, cocoa, baking powder, and salt.

In a large bowl, combine the butter or margarine, cream cheese, and sugar. With an electric mixer on medium speed, beat for 2 minutes, or until smooth. One at a time, add the egg and egg whites, beating after each addition until smooth. Add the vanilla extract. Beat just to incorporate.

Reduce the mixer speed to low. Gradually add the flour mixture, beating just to combine. With a spoon, stir in the walnuts. Pour the batter into the prepared pan.

Bake for 30 minutes, or until a wooden pick inserted in the center comes out almost clean. Remove to a rack to cool.

Makes 24 brownies

Per brownie: *116 calories, 2 g protein, 18 g carbohydrates, 5 g fat, 15 mg cholesterol, 50 mg sodium, 1 g dietary fiber*

Diet Exchanges: *0 milk, 0 vegetable, 0 fruit, 1 bread, 0 meat, 1 fat*

Super-Easy Blueberry Topped Angel Food Cake

—Debra Baum, Albany, New York

"This is a delicious way to enjoy a fat-free dessert loaded with wonderful antioxidant blueberries."

2 cups blueberries

2 tablespoons sugar

2 teaspoons ground cinnamon

1 sugar-free or regular angel food cake

2 cups fat-free or lite frozen whipped topping, thawed

Combine the blueberries, sugar, and cinnamon in a microwaveable bowl and microwave on high power for 45 to 60 seconds.

Cut the cake into 8 slices and place on dessert dishes. Evenly divide the blueberry mixture and the whipped topping among the slices.

Makes 8 servings

Per serving: *173 calories, 3 g protein, 39 g carbohydrates, 1 g fat, 0 mg cholesterol, 331 mg sodium, 2 g dietary fiber*

Diet Exchanges: *0 milk, 0 vegetable, 0 fruit, ½ bread, 0 meat, 0 fat*

Pineapple Angel Food Cake

—Kathleen Latcham, Rochester, Minnesota

"This cake is easy, and portions are generous yet low in calories. I can serve this recipe to dinner guests. Sometimes I top the cake with a few strawberries."

1 angel food cake mix (the one-step type mix)

1 can (20 ounces) crushed unsweetened pineapple in juice

1 teaspoon grated orange peel

Preheat the oven to 350°F.

Prepare the cake mix according to package directions, adding the pineapple (with juice) and orange peel in place of the water. Pour into an ungreased

13" × 9" baking pan or 10" tube pan.

Bake for 35 to 45 minutes, or until golden brown.

Makes 12 servings

Per serving: *167 calories, 4 g protein, 39 g carbohydrates, 0 g fat, 0 mg cholesterol, 374 mg sodium, 0 g dietary fiber*

Diet Exchanges: *0 milk, 0 vegetable, 1 fruit, 2 bread, 0 meat, 0 fat*

It Worked for Me!

Ann Hirschy

VITAL STATS

Weight lost: 50 pounds

Time to goal: 18 months

Unique secret to success: Paying careful attention to the textures and flavors of favorite foods, then substituting more healthful alternatives

Focusing really helped Ann get a handle on weight loss—from taking the time to savor the foods she ate to taking note of her reasons for eating.

"I was 38 years old, weighed 197 pounds, and was looking ahead to my 40th birthday. I really wanted to be happy with my weight when I reached that milestone. It was November of 1999, and my big birthday was coming up on July 13, 2001—that gave me about 20 months to get to '140 by 40.'

"I noticed that I tend to eat more when I'm upset or under stress. Keeping a food diary was a good way to track all of the little nibbles and tastes of food that I took in each day without even realizing it. Soon, the diary served as an alternative to eating just for comfort.

"I also allowed myself one 'free' meal a week—in moderation—such as dinner with my family at a buffet restaurant. This was a great way to feel my success because I could finally eat just one plate of salad, one plate of hot foods, and a small sampling of the dessert bar and feel satisfied. Before I started

to focus on losing weight, I felt that I wasn't getting my money's worth unless I gorged myself with two plates of everything.

"One of the most important things I learned is to pay attention to the flavors and textures of foods I really enjoy, then substitute a more healthful food for the fattening foods I tend to overeat. For example, when I crave chocolate, rather than indulging in a double-fudge brownie with ice cream and chocolate syrup, I have a cup of fat-free hot chocolate. The difference in calories, fat, and guilt are well worth it. I've even switched to cheeses and butter substitutes made from lower-fat vegetable protein.

"I also did my best to balance eating sensibly with enough exercise. I swim, take a Spinning class, and run. I also do yoga to help with a hamstring injury. And I try to lift weights 1 to 3 days a week. I'm trying these days to get back into doing the types of fun exercise I enjoyed as a teenager, such as skiing. This past ski season I really enjoyed being in shape enough and having the endurance to ski hard the whole time without having to stop several times per run."

Peppermint Patty Cake

266 Calories

CAKE

- 6 egg whites
- 1½ cups sugar
- 2 egg yolks
- ⅔ cup pureed baby-food prunes or prune butter
- ½ cup water
- ⅓ cup buttermilk
- 2 tablespoons canola oil
- 2 teaspoons instant coffee powder
- ¼ teaspoon peppermint extract
- 1 cup unbleached all-purpose flour
- ¾ cup unsweetened cocoa powder
- 2 teaspoons baking powder
- 1 teaspoon baking soda
- ⅛ teaspoon salt

ICING

- 1 cup confectioners' sugar
- 2 tablespoons fat-free milk
- ⅛ teaspoon peppermint extract
- 2 cups fat-free frozen whipped topping, thawed

To make the cake:

Preheat the oven to 350°F. Coat a 13" × 9" baking dish with cooking spray.

Place the egg whites in a large bowl. With an electric mixer on medium speed, beat until soft peaks form. Gradually add ½ cup of the sugar and continue to beat until the whites are firm and glossy.

In a small bowl, combine the egg yolks, prune puree, water, buttermilk, oil, coffee powder, and peppermint extract. In a large bowl, combine the flour, cocoa, baking powder, baking soda, salt, and the remaining 1 cup sugar. Add the prune mixture and stir until just moistened; do not overmix. Fold in the beaten egg whites and pour into the prepared baking dish. Bake for 25 minutes, or until a wooden pick inserted in the center comes out clean. Cool completely in the pan.

To make the icing:

In a medium bowl, combine the confectioners' sugar, milk, and peppermint extract until smooth. Fold in the whipped topping. Spread over the cooled cake. Refrigerate for 2 hours.

Makes 12 servings

Per serving: *266 calories, 5 g protein, 52 g carbohydrates, 5 g fat, 35 mg cholesterol, 260 mg sodium, 2 g dietary fiber*

Diet Exchanges: *0 milk, 0 vegetable, 0 fruit, 3 bread, ½ meat, 1 fat*

Chocolate Cake with Fluffy Chocolate Icing

308 Calories

CAKE

1½ cups unbleached all-purpose flour

½ cup unsweetened cocoa powder

1 tablespoon instant espresso powder

1 teaspoon baking soda

½ cup butter or margarine, softened

1 cup sugar

1 egg

1 teaspoon vanilla extract

½ cup buttermilk

½ cup hot water

ICING

1½ cups sugar

3 large egg whites

¼ cup water

1 teaspoon cream of tartar

1 teaspoon vanilla extract

¼ cup unsweetened cocoa powder

Semisweet chocolate curls

To make the cake:

Preheat the oven to 350°F. Coat 2 (8") round cake pans with cooking spray.

In a medium bowl, combine the flour, cocoa, espresso powder, and baking soda.

In a large bowl, with an electric mixer on medium speed, beat the butter or margarine and sugar for 3 minutes, or until creamy. Add the egg and vanilla extract and beat on low speed until creamy. With the mixer on low speed, gradually add the flour mixture, alternating with the buttermilk and water.

Pour the batter into the prepared pans. Bake for 25 minutes, or until a wooden pick inserted in the center comes out clean. Cool on racks for 5 minutes. Invert the cakes onto the racks and cool completely.

To make the icing:

Meanwhile, in the top of a double boiler, combine the sugar, egg whites, water, and cream of tartar. Place over a saucepan of simmering water. With an electric mixer on high speed, beat for 5 minutes, or until soft peaks form. Add the vanilla extract and beat for 4 minutes, or until the mixture is thick and glossy and registers 160°F on an instant-read thermometer. Remove from the heat. Sift the cocoa over the frosting and gently fold in. Cool completely, about 20 minutes.

Place one cake layer on a serving plate. Spread the top with icing. Top with the remaining cake layer. Spread the top with icing. Spread the remaining icing over the sides. Garnish with the chocolate, if using.

Makes 12 servings

Per serving: *308 calories, 4 g protein, 56 g carbohydrates, 9 g fat, 40 mg cholesterol, 210 mg sodium, 2 g dietary fiber*

Diet Exchanges: *0 milk, 0 vegetable, 0 fruit, 3 bread, 0 meat, 1½ fat*

Chocolate Cheesecake

—Brandye Ranum, Baker, Montana

*" I love cheesecake, and the soy version has heart-healthy isoflavones.
I have served this at family gatherings, and they can't tell when it's nondairy—they love it! "*

1½ cups chocolate cookie crumbs, finely crushed

2 tablespoons butter or margarine, melted

32 ounces low-fat cream cheese or soy cream cheese

1¼ cups sugar

2 eggs

1 egg white

6 ounces chocolate chips, melted and cooled slightly

1 cup soy sour cream

1 teaspoon vanilla extract

Preheat the oven to 325°F.

In a small bowl, combine the cookie crumbs and margarine. Press into the bottom of a 9" springform pan.

In a large bowl, with an electric mixer on medium speed, combine the cream cheese and sugar until well-blended. Add the eggs, one at a time, and egg white, beating well after each addition. Add the melted chocolate chips, sour cream, and vanilla extract and beat just until blended. Pour over the prepared crust.

Bake for 1 hour 25 minutes. Turn off the oven and leave in the oven for 1 hour. Remove to a rack to cool completely.

Makes 20 servings

Per serving: *269 calories, 7 g protein, 27 g carbohydrates, 15 g fat, 50 mg cholesterol, 250 mg sodium, 1 g dietary fiber*

Diet Exchanges: *0 milk, 0 vegetable, 0 fruit, 1½ bread, 0 meat, 2½ fat*

Kitchen Tip

For a fruity variation, try stirring ⅓ cup raspberry jam into the mix. Berry delicious!

No-Bake Lemon Cheesecake

—**Norma Layton, Lincoln, Nebraska**

"This cheesecake is satisfying when I want something sweet."

12 **graham cracker squares, coarsely chopped**

 2 **tablespoons butter or margarine, melted**

½ **cup boiling water**

 1 **package (4-serving size) sugar-free lemon gelatin**

 3 **ounces reduced-fat cream cheese, softened and cut into cubes**

 1 **lemon**

 2 **cups reduced-fat sour cream**

 8 **ounces lite frozen whipped topping, thawed**

 Sliced strawberries for garnish

In a small bowl, combine the graham cracker pieces and butter or margarine. Press into the bottom of a 9" springform pan.

In a medium bowl, combine the water and gelatin; stir until the gelatin is dissolved. Add the cream cheese and stir until dissolved.

Grate 1 teaspoon peel from the lemon and add to the gelatin mixture. Squeeze the juice from the lemon (about 3 tablespoons) and add to the gelatin mixture. Add the sour cream and whipped topping and stir to combine.

Pour over the crust and smooth the top. Chill in the refrigerator for 30 minutes, or until set. Arrange the strawberries on top of the cheesecake.

Makes 10 servings

Per serving: *223 calories, 13 g protein, 14 g carbohydrates, 15 g fat, 50 mg cholesterol, 140 mg sodium, 1 g dietary fiber*

Diet Exchanges: *0 milk, 0 vegetable, 0 fruit, 1 bread, ½ meat, 2½ fat*

CURB CRAVINGS WITH FUN

If you've ever lost control over a dessert, you may need more good times, not more willpower. One study suggests that dopamine, a neurochemical that helps regulate mood and appetite, may be deficient in overweight people, leading them to overeat to boost their spirits.

Researchers aren't sure if overeaters are born with fewer dopamine receptors or if bingeing eventually causes the brain to tone down its response to food. Luckily, you can boost dopamine in other ways besides eating—by exercising, socializing, making love, even riding roller coasters, says study author Gene Jack-Wang, M.D., of Brookhaven National Laboratory in Upton, New York. Instead of dining out with your spouse, take a walk together, he says. "You're exercising, taming your appetite, and building your relationship all at once."

French Apple Cake

—Barbara Willison, Howells, Nebraska

"This recipe allows me to enjoy a sweet treat without a lot of calories. The nutritional value of the apples is an added plus."

⅓ cup packed brown sugar

1 tablespoon unbleached all-purpose flour

½ teaspoon ground cinnamon

2 tablespoons light butter or margarine, melted

1 tablespoon lemon juice or orange juice

3 apples peeled, cored, and sliced

1 fat-free white cake mix

Fat-free frozen whipped topping, thawed, for garnish

Preheat the oven to 350°F. Coat a 13" × 9" baking pan with cooking spray.

In a large bowl, combine the brown sugar, flour, and cinnamon. Sprinkle over the bottom of the prepared baking pan.

In a cup, combine the margarine and lemon juice or orange juice. Place the apples in the pan and drizzle with the butter mixture.

Prepare the cake mix according to package directions. Pour over the apple mixture.

Bake for 30 minutes, or until a wooden pick inserted in the center comes out clean. Cool for 20 minutes. Invert onto a serving platter or tray. Serve with the whipped topping.

Makes 12 servings

Per serving: *267 calories, 2 g protein, 51 g carbohydrates, 6 g fat, 0 mg cholesterol, 326 mg sodium, 1 g dietary fiber*

Diet Exchanges: *0 milk, 0 vegetable, 0 fruit, 3 bread, 0 meat, 1 fat*

SECRETS OF WEIGHT-LOSS WINNERS

• I eat one hot-from-the-oven cookie with a filling glass of milk. As soon as the rest cool, I package them up.

—Jennifer Becker,
Tempe, Arizona

• I tell myself I'd rather feel energetic than sluggish. So when the urge to eat strikes, I reach for my dumbbells instead of the cookie jar.

—Paula George, Baltimore, Maryland

• Instead of having my own dessert, I nibble my husband's. One bite cures my craving.

—Wendy Hooten, Garland, Texas

FOR LONG-LASTING RESULTS

You don't have to swear off cheese-cake or eat carrot sticks nonstop to see permanent changes. Participants in a 3-year German diet project who trimmed at least 5 percent of their body weight and kept it off more than a year have some practical and even enjoyable habits in common. Experienced weight maintainers:

Sit down to eat. Take the time for three or four meals (about 500 calories each for a 140-pound woman) and snack only when you're hungry.

Use shopping lists to avoid fattening impulse buys. Also peruse the produce section, check labels, and generally eat a nutritious diet.

Enjoy chocolate guilt-free. But limit intake to two candy bars a week.

Relieve stress by learning alternative ways of coping. Walk or talk with a friend instead of munching on potato chips.

Dance, bicycle, join a softball team— whatever it takes to make exercise pleasurable.

Aren't on a diet one day and off the next. A healthy lifestyle takes time.

Sweetheart Cherry Pie

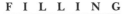

216 Calories

FILLING

- 4 cups pitted sour cherries
- ½ cup maple syrup
- 3 tablespoons quick-cooking tapioca
- 1 teaspoon ground cinnamon

CRUST

- 1 cup cake flour
- ¼ cup butter or margarine, cut into small pieces
- 1 egg white

To make the filling:

In a 2-quart saucepan over medium heat, combine the cherries, maple syrup, tapioca, and cinnamon. Let stand for 5 minutes. Cook, stirring occasionally, for 10 minutes.

To make the crust:

Preheat the oven to 400°F.

Place the flour in a medium bowl. Using 2 knives, cut in the butter or margarine until the mixture resembles coarse meal. Stir in the egg white. Place on a lightly floured surface and knead for 30 seconds, or until smooth. Reserve ¼ cup of the dough.

Place the remaining dough between sheets of waxed paper and roll into a 9" circle. Remove the top piece of waxed paper. Invert the dough onto an 8" pie plate. Remove the remaining piece of waxed paper and fit the dough into the pie plate. Fold under the excess pastry and crimp the edges. Prick the bottom of the dough and bake for 10 minutes.

Roll the reserved dough between sheets of waxed paper to ⅛" thickness. Using a cookie cutter, cut out hearts or other decorative shapes. Pour the cherry filling into the pie crust and arrange the cutouts on top.

Reduce the oven temperature to 350°F. Bake for 30 minutes.

Makes 8 servings

Per serving: *216 calories, 3 g protein, 39 g carbohydrates, 6 g fat, 15 mg cholesterol, 70 mg sodium, 2 g dietary fiber*

Diet Exchanges: *0 milk, 0 vegetable, ½ fruit, 1½ bread, 0 meat, 1 fat*

Kitchen Tip

You may use frozen sour cherries that have been thawed instead of fresh cherries.

Key Lime Pie

380 Calories

CRUST

- 1 egg white
- 1½ cups crumbled gingersnap cookies (about 30)
- 1 tablespoon + 1½ teaspoons butter or margarine, melted
- 1 tablespoon + 1½ teaspoons canola oil

FILLING

- ½ cup lime juice
- 1 tablespoon grated lime rind
- 1 can (14 ounces) fat-free sweetened condensed milk
- 2 egg yolks
- ½ cup sugar
- 1 teaspoon cornstarch
- 4 large egg whites
- ¼ teaspoon cream of tartar

To make the crust:

Preheat the oven to 375°F. Coat a 9" pie plate with cooking spray.

Place the egg white in a medium bowl and beat lightly with a fork. Add the gingersnaps, butter or margarine, and oil and blend well. Pour into the prepared pie plate and press in an even layer on the bottom and up the sides. Bake for 8 to 10 minutes, or until lightly browned and firm. Cool on a rack.

To make the filling:

In a large bowl, combine the lime juice, lime rind, condensed milk, and egg yolks.

In a small bowl, combine the sugar and cornstarch. Place the egg whites and cream of tartar in a medium bowl. With an electric mixer on medium speed, beat until foamy. Increase the speed to high and gradually beat in the sugar mixture. Continue to beat until the whites are firm and glossy. Fold ¾ cup of the meringue into the lime mixture. Pour into the prepared crust and bake for 15 minutes. Remove from the oven.

Spoon the remaining meringue over the filling and spread to the edges of the crust. Using the spoon, make small peaks in the meringue. Bake for 10 minutes, or until the meringue is golden brown and set. (If the meringue browns too quickly, reduce the oven temperature to 350°F.) Cool completely on a rack. Refrigerate for 1 to 2 hours.

Makes 10 servings

Per serving: *380 calories, 9 g protein, 69 g carbohydrates, 8 g fat, 50 mg cholesterol, 300 mg sodium, 0 g dietary fiber*

Diet Exchanges: *0 milk, 0 vegetable, 0 fruit, 4½ bread, ½ meat, 1 fat*

Kitchen Tip

Experiment with different kinds of low-fat cookie crusts. Try using crushed low-fat vanilla or chocolate wafers or cinnamon graham crackers.

Lite Banana Cream Pie

—**Kim Fuller, Laurel, Maryland**

"I have desperate cravings for sweets. This pie is light, creamy, and delicious. A wonderful guilt-free pleasure. Just what I need to stay on course."

2   **bananas, sliced**
    Juice of 1 lemon
1   **prepared 9" reduced-fat graham cracker pie crust**
10 **ounces fat-free banana yogurt**
1   **container (8 ounces) lite frozen whipped topping, thawed**

Place the bananas in a small bowl and drizzle with the lemon juice. Arrange in a single layer in the prepared crust; reserve any remaining banana slices for garnish.

In a medium bowl, combine the yogurt and whipped topping. Evenly spread over the bananas. Garnish with the remaining banana slices. Chill before serving.

Makes 10 servings

Per serving: *205 calories, 2 g protein, 29 g carbohydrates, 9 g fat, 0 mg cholesterol, 152 mg sodium, 1 g dietary fiber*

Diet Exchanges: *0 milk, 0 vegetable, ½ fruit, 1 bread, 0 meat, 1½ fat*

A BETTER WAY TO SUPERSIZE

Filling up on more food may be a better way to cut calories. Researchers asked 28 men to drink a strawberry milk shake before a buffet lunch on three different days. The shakes contained exactly the same ingredients and number of calories, but they were blended differently to incorporate more or less air so that each one had a different volume: filling half, three-quarters, or a full glass.

After drinking the "biggest" shake, the men ate 100 fewer calories at lunch and reported less hunger compared with when they drank the "smallest" shake. And they didn't make up for it at dinner, so they trimmed 100 calories off their day's total.

Pumping up the volume of foods means you get to eat more, and making food look bigger satisfies your desire to have a filling portion. So feel free to enjoy more "airy" foods that fill your plate, such as angel food cake, fruit smoothies, low-calorie ice creams, mousses, and meringues. For extra appeal, serve high-volume desserts in clear glasses so you can see just how much you're getting. And add height with a dollop of low-fat whipped topping.

Pumpkin Pie

—Jill Williams, Chattahoochee, Florida

"I'm a Weight Watcher, and this recipe has helped me have a dessert for low points."

1 can (15 ounces) pumpkin
½ cup packed brown sugar substitute
½ cup packed regular brown sugar
1 tablespoon molasses
1¼ teaspoons ground cinnamon
¾ teaspoon ground ginger
¼ teaspoon salt
⅛ teaspoon ground allspice
¾ cup liquid egg substitute
1 cup fat-free evaporated milk
1 prepared 9" reduced-fat graham cracker pie crust
½ cup fat-free frozen whipped topping, thawed

Preheat the oven to 425°F.

In a large bowl, combine the pumpkin, brown sugars, molasses, cinnamon, ginger, salt, and allspice. Add the egg substitute and milk and mix thoroughly. Pour into the prepared crust.

Bake for 45 minutes, or until a wooden pick inserted in the center comes out clean. Cool on a rack. Garnish with the whipped topping.

Makes 10 servings

Per serving: *240 calories, 6 g protein, 41 g carbohydrates, 6 g fat, 4 mg cholesterol, 280 mg sodium, 2 g dietary fiber*

Diet Exchanges: *½ milk, 0 vegetable, 0 fruit, 3 bread, ½ meat, 1 fat*

Pear and Cranberry Crisp

240 Calories

FILLING

- 1 lemon
- 8 pears, cut into ½" slices
- 1 cup dried cranberries
- ⅔ cup sugar
- ⅔ cup pear nectar or apple juice
- 3 tablespoons unbleached all-purpose flour

TOPPING

- ⅔ cup quick-cooking rolled oats
- ⅓ cup packed light brown sugar
- ¼ cup unbleached all-purpose flour
- 1 teaspoon ground cinnamon
- 2 tablespoons butter or margarine, melted

To make the filling:

Preheat the oven to 375°F. Coat a 1½-quart baking dish with cooking spray.

Grate 1 teaspoon rind from the lemon into a large bowl. Cut the lemon in half and squeeze the juice into the bowl; discard the lemon. Add the pears and toss to coat. Stir in the cranberries, sugar, pear nectar or apple juice, and flour. Mix well and spoon into the prepared baking dish.

To make the topping:

In a small bowl, combine the oats, brown sugar, flour, cinnamon, and butter or margarine. Sprinkle over the filling. Bake for 40 minutes, or until the filling is bubbling and the top is browned. Serve warm or at room temperature.

Makes 8 servings

Per serving: *240 calories, 2 g protein, 51 g carbohydrates, 4 g fat, 0 mg cholesterol, 5 mg sodium, 2 g dietary fiber*

Diet Exchanges: *0 milk, 0 vegetable, 1 fruit, 2 bread, 0 meat, ½ fat*

Kitchen Tip

To make a summer crisp, substitute fresh peaches for the pears, pitted Bing cherries or blueberries for the cranberries, and apricot nectar for the pear nectar.

Apple Crisp

—Loise DiPalma, Wallingford, Connecticut

"This is a great dessert to serve to company.
They won't even know that it's healthy, and it's super-fast and easy."

4 **large Granny Smith apples, peeled and cut into ¼" slices**

1 **can (16 ounces) whole cranberries**

1 **tablespoon unbleached all-purpose flour**

1 **cup rolled oats (not quick-cooking)**

2 **tablespoons sugar**

1 **teaspoon ground cinnamon**

¼ **cup walnuts**

4 **tablespoons applesauce**

   Fat-free frozen whipped topping, thawed

Preheat the oven to 325°F. Coat an 8" × 8" baking dish with cooking spray.

Place the apples in the prepared baking dish. Combine the cranberries with the flour and toss with the apples.

In a food processor, combine the oats, sugar, cinnamon, and walnuts. Pulse, gradually adding the applesauce until the mixture starts to clump. Spoon over the cranberries.

Bake for 45 minutes, or until the apples are tender and the topping is lightly browned. Cover with foil, if necessary, to prevent browning too quickly. Serve with whipped topping.

Makes 6 servings

Per serving: *250 calories, 2 g protein, 53 g carbohydrates, 3 g fat, 0 mg cholesterol, 29 mg sodium, 4 g dietary fiber*

Diet Exchanges: *0 milk, 0 vegetable, 1½ fruit, 1½ bread, 0 meat, ½ fat*

SHOPPING SAVVY

Apples Away!

Would you eat more fruit if it was easier? Now you can enjoy grab-and-go apple slices without stopping to cut them or having the slices turn brown on you. Low-cal, no fat, plenty of fiber—the perfect prescription for weight loss. Crunch Pak apple slices are rinsed in FDA-approved NatureSeal (not a preservative), which stops oxidation, protecting the fruit's color, flavor, and crispness. The slices stay fresh in the refrigerator for up to 3 weeks. Choose from Fuji, Granny Smith, Pink Lady, Braeburn, and Gala. Look for them in the produce section.

Cherry Cobbler

—Colleen Rush, Cumming, Georgia

*"*This cobbler is low-calorie and satisfies my dessert craving.
It provides high-quality carbs, fruit, and dairy if you top it with yogurt!*"*

FILLING

1 package (16 ounces) frozen dark sweet cherries, thawed, or 1 can (20 ounces) cherry pie filling

⅛ teaspoon allspice

TOPPING

2 packets plain instant oatmeal

½ cup unbleached all-purpose flour

2 tablespoons sugar

1½ teaspoons baking powder

½ cup 1% milk

¼ teaspoon cherry extract or vanilla extract

1 cup fat-free vanilla or cherry vanilla frozen yogurt (optional)

To make the filling:

Coat an 8" × 8" baking dish with cooking spray. Add the cherries, sprinkle with the allspice, and stir.

To make the topping:

Preheat the oven to 350°F.

In a medium bowl, combine the oatmeal, flour, sugar, baking powder, milk, and cherry extract or vanilla extract. Pour over the cherry mixture.

Bake for 30 minutes, or until the crust is golden and bubbly. Serve with the frozen yogurt, if using.

Makes 8 servings

Per serving: *164 calories, 4 g protein, 36 g carbohydrates, 1 g fat, 0 mg cholesterol, 180 mg sodium, 1 g dietary fiber*

Diet Exchanges: *0 milk, 0 vegetable, 1 fruit, 1 bread, 0 meat, 0 fat*

BEATING SNACK ATTACKS

A study of overweight women found that more than half ate 70 percent of their daily calories after 7 P.M.—mostly as health-busting foods high in fat, sugar, and calories. If this sounds familiar, these tips can help.

Store food out of sight. Stash supper leftovers, empty candy dishes, and remove snacks except fruit from countertops.

Defeat cravings with an egg timer. Wait 5 to 10 minutes to see if your snack attack simply passes. Work up to 15 to 20 minutes.

Go to bed. If all else fails, an early bedtime takes you out of temptation's way (and rewards you with extra sleep time).

Apricot Soufflé

213 Calories

4 ounces dried apricots
½ cup water
½ cup orange juice
½ cup sugar
2 teaspoons lemon juice
½ teaspoon vanilla extract
4 egg whites
¼ teaspoon cream of tartar
Pinch of salt
1 tablespoon confectioners' sugar

In a medium saucepan over medium heat, combine the apricots, water, orange juice, and 3 tablespoons of the sugar. Cover and bring to a boil. Simmer for 15 minutes, or until the apricots are soft. Let cool for 5 minutes. Place in a food processor or blender and puree. Place in a bowl and stir in the lemon juice and vanilla extract. Let cool to room temperature.

Preheat the oven to 350°F. Coat four 6-ounce ramekins or custard cups with cooking spray. Use 2 tablespoons of the remaining sugar to coat the ramekins; tap out the excess. Place the ramekins on a baking sheet.

Place the egg whites, cream of tartar, and salt in a large bowl. With an electric mixer on medium speed, beat until foamy. Gradually beat in the remaining 3 tablespoons sugar. Increase the speed to high and continue to beat until the whites are firm and glossy.

Stir one-third of the egg-white mixture into the apricot puree. Gently fold in the remaining egg-white mixture until thoroughly incorporated. Spoon the mixture into the prepared ramekins and smooth the tops.

Bake for 20 minutes, or until puffed, golden brown, and just set in the center. Remove from the oven and sift the confectioners' sugar over the top. Serve immediately.

Makes 4 servings

Per serving: *213 calories, 5 g protein, 49 g carbohydrates, 0 g fat, 0 mg cholesterol, 65 mg sodium, 2 g dietary fiber*

Diet Exchanges: *0 milk, 0 vegetable, 1½ fruit, 1½ bread, ½ meat, 0 fat*

Kitchen Tip

The apricots can be cooked and pureed up to 4 days in advance and stored in the refrigerator in an airtight container. Bring the puree to room temperature before folding in the beaten egg whites.
This dish can also be made in a 1-quart soufflé dish. Increase the baking time to 30 to 35 minutes.

Tiramisu

299 Calories

1 tablespoons + 1½ teaspoons instant espresso powder or 3 tablespoons instant coffee powder

½ cup + 1½ tablespoons hot water

32 ladyfingers, split

3 tablespoons seedless raspberry jam

3 egg whites, at room temperature

1 cup + 2 tablespoons sugar

3 tablespoons cold water

¼ teaspoon cream of tartar

4 ounces mascarpone cheese

4 ounces reduced-fat cream cheese, at room temperature

1 tablespoon semisweet chocolate shavings

Preheat the oven to 350°F.

In a small bowl, combine the espresso or coffee powder and ½ cup of the hot water. Brush the cut side of each ladyfinger with the mixture.

In another small bowl, combine the jam with the remaining 1½ tablespoons hot water to make a spreadable mixture. Brush the top side of each ladyfinger with a light coating of the mixture.

Bring about 2" water to a simmer in a large saucepan. In a medium heatproof bowl that will fit over the saucepan, combine the egg whites, sugar, cold water, and cream of tartar. Place the bowl over the saucepan. With an electric mixer on low speed, beat for

5 minutes. Increase the speed to high and beat for 4 minutes longer, or until very thick. Remove the bowl from the saucepan. Beat for 4 minutes, or until the mixture is very light and fluffy.

In a large bowl, combine the mascarpone and cream cheese. Using the same mixer, beat until creamy. Add 1 cup of the egg-white mixture and beat until smooth. Gradually fold in the remaining egg-white mixture.

Line the bottom and sides of a 2-quart serving bowl or a 9" × 9" baking dish with 16 of the ladyfingers, jam side up; top with one-fourth of the filling. Repeat 3 times to use all the ladyfingers and filling. Sprinkle with the chocolate.

Cover and refrigerate for at least 4 hours or up to 3 days before serving.

Makes 10 servings

Per serving: *299 calories, 6 g protein, 48 g carbohydrates, 10 g fat, 78 mg cholesterol, 330 mg sodium, 0 g dietary fiber*

Diet Exchanges: *0 milk, 0 vegetable, 0 fruit, 3 bread, ½ meat, 1½ fat*

Kitchen Tip

Mascarpone is a dense Italian triple-cream cheese made from cow's milk and is available in Italian markets and some supermarkets.

It Worked for Me!

Debra Whitfield

VITAL STATS

Weight lost: 60 pounds

Time to goal: 1 year

Unique secret to success:
Going completely vegetarian immediately eliminated a substantial amount of fat and calories, allowing her to start losing weight without even trying

Opting for a nontraditional form of exercise—becoming a massage therapist—allows Debra to get a toning, calorie-burning, hour-long workout and get paid at the same time.

"Two years ago, I visited my family doctor to get advice on what I thought might be a thyroid condition. When the blood tests came back, I found out that my thyroid was normal—but my cholesterol and blood sugar levels were much too high.

"My doctor gave me 6 months to get my levels down on my own, through weight loss and changing my diet. Otherwise, he said, I'd need to take medication, which definitely was not an option for me. I have family members who rely on drugs for diabetes and high blood pressure, and I did not want to have to deal with the side effects they suffer from.

"Right around that time, I started to read about the health benefits of eating a vegetarian diet. I did some research and made the decision to stop eating meat altogether.

"Going vegetarian really limited my fast-food choices and encouraged me to eat more vegetables. Instead of the usual cooking methods like boiling or steaming, I bought a countertop grilling appliance and learned to grill my veggies with a little olive oil—they're extra delicious that way. I also started eating fruit, something I couldn't stand before. Now, rather than sitting down to eat an apple (just too boring for me), I take the time to slice up a variety of fruits and make a fruit salad. I find the combination of flavors and textures much more interesting and satisfying to eat.

"I'm a nurse part-time, so deciding to learn massage therapy was not that much of a stretch. Basically, I wanted to find a form of exercise that didn't require going outside in the Texas heat and also didn't have to happen in a gym. It's a bonus that I can get paid for doing it. And giving a massage is a serious workout—in particular, it really helps keep your chest from going south. My bust has actually shrunk by one cup size, and the muscles in my chest and arms are much more toned now."

Persimmon Pudding

—Yvonne Rios, Lake Elsinore, California

"I use whole wheat pastry flour in this pudding to kick the fiber up."

½ **cup whole wheat pastry flour**

1 **cup raisins (optional)**

½ **cup sugar**

¼ **cup nuts, such as almonds or pecans, finely chopped**

1 **teaspoon baking soda**

¾ **teaspoon ground cinnamon**

½ **teaspoon salt**

1 **cup persimmon pulp**

½ **cup 2% milk**

1 **egg**

1 **teaspoon vanilla extract**

In a large bowl, combine the flour, raisins (if using), sugar, nuts, baking soda, cinnamon, and salt. Add the persimmon pulp, milk, egg, and vanilla extract and stir to combine. Place in an 8" × 8" baking dish and bake for 45 minutes.

Makes 6 servings

Per serving: *197 calories, 4 g protein, 37 g carbohydrates, 4 g fat, 35 mg cholesterol, 430 mg sodium, 2 g dietary fiber*

Diet Exchanges: *0 milk, 0 vegetable, 1 fruit, 1 bread, ½ meat, ½ fat*

Kitchen Tip

Look for persimmons between October and February. The fruit should be soft yet firm, and will keep in the refrigerator for up to 3 days.

Chocolate Pudding Crunch

—Jay Brown, Gonzales, Texas

"This snack takes only a few seconds to prepare. It's so delicious, you just can't believe that it's nutritious, too!"

1 **container (8 ounces) fat-free chocolate pudding**

½ **cup all-bran cereal**

1 **teaspoon coconut extract**

In a medium bowl, combine the pudding, cereal, and coconut extract. Stir to mix.

Makes 1 serving

Per serving: *303 calories, 10 g protein, 71 carbohydrates, 2 g fat, 5 mg cholesterol, 674 mg sodium, 13 g dietary fiber*

Diet Exchanges: *0 milk, 0 vegetable, 0 fruit, 1 bread, 0 meat, 0 fat*

Kitchen Tip

If you like, you can also stir a handful of raisins into the pudding.

Chocolate Mousse

 176 Calories

- ¾ cup 1% milk
- 1 tablespoon instant coffee powder
- ⅔ cup unsweetened cocoa powder
- ¼ cup packed light brown sugar
- 1 egg, lightly beaten
- 2 tablespoons coffee liqueur or strong brewed coffee
- 1 teaspoon unflavored gelatin
- 2 ounces bittersweet chocolate, coarsely chopped
- 1 tablespoon vanilla extract
- 4 egg whites
- ½ cup sugar
- ½ teaspoon cream of tartar
- 1 cup fat-free frozen whipped topping, thawed + additional for garnish (optional)

In a medium saucepan, combine the milk and coffee powder. Cook, stirring occasionally, over medium heat for 2 minutes, or until steaming. Whisk in the cocoa and brown sugar until smooth. Remove from the heat and slowly whisk in the egg. Reduce the heat to low and whisk constantly for 5 minutes, or until thickened. Remove from the heat.

Place the coffee liqueur or coffee in a cup. Sprinkle with the gelatin. Let stand for 1 minute to soften. Stir into the cocoa mixture until dissolved. Add the chocolate and vanilla extract and stir until the chocolate is melted. Place in a large bowl and set aside for 30 min-

utes, or until cooled to room temperature.

Bring 2" water to a simmer in a medium saucepan. In a large heatproof bowl that will fit over the saucepan, whisk together the egg whites, sugar, and cream of tartar. Set the bowl over the simmering water and gently whisk for 2 minutes, or until an instant-read thermometer registers 140°F (the mixture will be too hot to touch). Remove from the heat.

With an electric mixer on medium-high speed, beat for 5 minutes, or until cool. Fold the egg-white mixture into the chocolate mixture. Fold in the whipped topping. Divide among dessert glasses and refrigerate for at least 2 hours or up to 24 hours. Garnish with additional whipped topping, if using.

Makes 8 servings

Per serving: *176 calories, 5 g protein, 26 g carbohydrates, 5 g fat, 25 mg cholesterol, 55 mg sodium, 3 g dietary fiber*

Diet Exchanges: *0 milk, 0 vegetable, 0 fruit, 1½ bread, ½ meat, 1 fat*

Kitchen Tip

This mousse also makes a wonderful filling for cakes and pies. One recipe is enough to fill a 9" layer cake (between the 2 cake layers). For a 9" pie shell, double the recipe. Prebake a graham cracker or chocolate crumb pie crust, fill with the mousse, and refrigerate for at least 2 hours before serving.

Yogurt Parfaits

—Rejeana Ebert, Tomahawk, Wisconsin

166 Calories

"I put this in fancy sherbet glasses and serve with whipped topping. This makes it seem extra special when you are on a lower-carb diet and are feeling dessert deprived! I love getting the goodness of plain yogurt without all the sugars I don't want."

1 package (4-serving size) sugar-free flavored gelatin

1 cup boiling water

1 cup low-fat plain yogurt

4 tablespoons frozen whipped topping, thawed

2 tablespoons chopped almonds

In a medium bowl, combine the gelatin and water and stir to dissolve. Add the yogurt and, with an electric mixer on medium speed, whip until smooth and creamy. Evenly divide among 4 parfait glasses and chill for 1 hour, or until firm. Top with the whipped topping and almonds.

Makes 4 servings

Per serving: *166 calories, 28 g protein, 6 g carbohydrates, 4 g fat, 5 mg cholesterol, 100 mg sodium, 1 g dietary fiber*

Diet Exchanges: *½ milk, 0 vegetable, 0 fruit, 0 bread, 2½ meat, 1 fat*

Chocolate-Raspberry Cooler

—Barbara Gibbs, Brooklyn

200 Calories

"This recipe helps satisfy my taste for chocolate in a low-fat, low-calorie way."

2 cups fat-free plain yogurt

2 teaspoons honey or 2 packets of stevia sweetener

¼ teaspoon vanilla extract

¼ cup chocolate sorbet

¼ cup raspberry sorbet

2 teaspoons chopped almonds or other nuts or seeds (optional)

In a medium bowl, combine the yogurt, honey or sweetener, and vanilla extract.

Evenly divide the chocolate sorbet and the raspberry sorbet between 2 dessert bowls.

Top with the yogurt mixture and sprinkle with the nuts, if using.

Makes 2 servings

Per serving: *200 calories, 11 g protein, 40 g carbohydrates, 1 g fat, 5 mg cholesterol, 150 mg sodium, 1 g dietary fiber*

Diet Exchanges: *1 milk, 0 vegetable, 0 fruit, 1½ bread, 0 meat, ½ fat*

Kitchen Tip

If you like, try freezing this dessert for an hour before serving to give the yogurt a wonderfully icy texture.

Frozen Fruit Dessert

—Kimberly Bryant, Tampa

*"If you like fruit as much as I do, you'll really enjoy this super-easy treat.
It has a texture similar to ice cream, and it's cold and sweet—great in summer!
This satisfies my ice cream and Popsicle cravings and helps prevent me from eating
those fat- and calorie-filled treats, which results in weight lost!"*

Sugar (optional)
2 **cups frozen berries, such as blueberries and/or raspberries (not thawed)**
1 **banana, broken into 4 pieces**
    Mint leaves, lemon or lime wedges, or banana slices, for garnish (optional)

Wet the rims of 2 frosty glasses with water and dip in the sugar, if using. Place both glasses in the freezer for 15 minutes.

Meanwhile, in a food processor or blender, combine the berries and banana and process until it's the consistency of soft ice cream. Place the mixture in the freezer for 15 minutes. Evenly divide between the glasses and garnish with the mint leaves, lemon or lime wedges, or banana slices, if using. Serve immediately.

Makes 2 servings

Per serving: *134 calories, 1 g protein, 33 g carbohydrates, 1 g fat, 0 mg cholesterol, 0 mg sodium, 6 g dietary fiber*

Diet Exchanges: *0 milk, 0 vegetable, 2 fruit, 0 bread, 0 meat, 0 fat*

FOR THOSE WHO LOVE DESSERT

You can satisfy your sweet tooth with fewer calories if you make the right choices.

Most fruits and some vegetables are naturally sweet, so take advantage of these low-calorie treasures. Rich fruits such as mango and banana are especially thick and creamy, while grapes and strawberries can be frozen for a snack that lasts longer and tastes sweeter. Other foods, such as yogurt, jams, some light cheeses, and foods spiced with cinnamon or vanilla extract, can add instant pleasure to a meal.

But the decadent sweets you also crave—chocolate, cheesecake, ice cream—have their place in weight loss, too. If you keep portions reasonable and look for lower-calorie options, you can have dessert every day.

Sherbet Dessert

—**Norma Layton, Lincoln, Nebraska**

"This dessert is really refreshing."

2 cups graham cracker crumbs +
  additional for topping
2 tablespoons butter or margarine, melted
½ gallon sherbet (any flavor), softened
2 containers (16 ounces) lite frozen
  whipped topping, thawed

Preheat the oven to 350°F.

In a 13" × 9" baking pan, combine the cracker crumbs and butter or margarine. Press into the bottom of the pan and bake for 7 minutes. Cool.

In a large bowl, thoroughly combine the sherbet and whipped topping. Evenly spread over the crust and dust with the remaining cracker crumbs. Freeze for 2 hours, or until firm.

Makes 12 servings

Per serving: *300 calories, 2 g protein, 49 g carbohydrates, 9 g fat, 10 mg cholesterol, 150 mg sodium, 0 g dietary fiber*

Diet Exchanges: *0 milk, 0 vegetable, 0 fruit, 3 bread, 0 meat, 1 fat*

Chilly Vanilla Ice Cream

—**Norma Layton, Lincoln, Nebraska**

"I always crave ice cream when trying to lose weight. This gives me great satisfaction."

1½ cups liquid egg substitute
3 cups sugar
3 cups thawed frozen creamer
1 tablespoon + 1½ teaspoons vanilla extract
4 cups 2% milk

In a large bowl, combine the egg substitute, sugar, creamer, and vanilla extract. Beat with an electric mixer on medium speed until smooth. Place in the container of a ½-gallon ice cream maker and fill to the freeze line with the milk. Freeze according to the manufacturer's instructions.

Makes 16 servings

Per serving: *273 calories, 4 g protein, 47 g carbohydrates, 7 g fat, 25 mg cholesterol, 85 mg sodium, 0 g dietary fiber*

Diet Exchanges: *0 milk, 0 vegetable, 0 fruit, 2½ bread, ½ meat, ½ fat*

Kitchen Tip

If using a 1-quart ice cream maker, halve the recipe.

Orange Fluff

—Judy Addington, Logan, Ohio

117 Calories

This treat tastes so good, you'll feel like you're cheating on your weight-loss efforts!

- 2 packages (0.3 ounces each) sugar-free orange gelatin
- 2 cups boiling water
- 1 cup low-fat cottage cheese
- 1 can (20 ounces) unsweetened crushed pineapple, drained
- 2 cans (11 ounces each) mandarin oranges, drained
- 1½ cups lite frozen whipped topping, thawed

In a medium bowl, combine the gelatin and water and stir until the gelatin dissolves. Add the cottage cheese, pineapple, and oranges. Chill until set. Spread with the whipped topping.

Makes 8 servings

Per serving: *117 calories, 5 g protein, 19 g carbohydrates, 2 g fat, 2 mg cholesterol, 99 mg sodium, 1 g dietary fiber*

Diet Exchanges: *0 milk, 0 vegetable, 1 fruit, 0 bread, ½ meat, ½ fat*

SHOPPING SAVVY

Tropical Mini-Fruit

Here's a convenient way to drop pounds: baby pineapples. They're quicker to process than full-size, and the pint-size fruit is sweeter, meatier, and juicier right down to the core. (Yes, that's edible too.) A serving of this Sugar Loaf variety has only 70 calories. Choose aromatic fruit with some yellow color in your grocer's produce section or order online at www.friedas.com.

Hearty Meals

Oven Dinners

Stove-Top Suppers

Side Dishes

Apricot-Stuffed Pork Loin

476 Calories

PORK LOIN

- ¾ cup wild rice
- 1½ teaspoons olive oil
- 1 onion, chopped
- 1 rib celery, chopped
- 1 clove garlic, minced
- 1 teaspoon dried thyme
- ¼ cup Madeira or fat-free chicken broth
- ½ cup chopped dried apricots
  Salt and black pepper
- 1 pork tenderloin (1½ pounds)

SAUCE

- 1 cup fat-free chicken broth
- ⅓ cup apricot nectar or orange juice
- 2 teaspoons Dijon mustard
- 2 teaspoons cornstarch
- 2 tablespoons water

To make the pork loin:

Prepare the wild rice according to package directions.

Meanwhile, heat the oil in a large nonstick skillet over medium heat. Add the onion, celery, garlic, and thyme and cook, stirring frequently, for 6 to 8 minutes, or until the onion is soft. Add the Madeira or broth and increase the heat to high. Cook for 2 minutes, or until the liquid is evaporated. Remove from the heat and stir in the apricots and wild rice. Season with salt and pepper.

With a knife, make a 1" slit from one end of the pork to the other, keeping the sides intact. Push the meat back from the slit to create a "tunnel." From both ends, stuff the cavity with the rice mixture. Mist the pork with cooking spray and season with salt and pepper.

Preheat the oven to 350°F. Heat a large ovenproof skillet coated with cooking spray over medium-high heat. Add the pork and cook for 4 minutes, or until browned on all sides. Place the skillet in the oven and cook for 25 minutes, or until a thermometer inserted in the center reaches 155°F and the juices run clear. Place on a cutting board. Let stand for 5 minutes before slicing.

To make the sauce:

In a small saucepan over medium-high heat, whisk together the broth, apricot nectar or orange juice, and mustard. Bring to a boil and cook for 2 minutes. Combine the cornstarch and water in a cup and stir until smooth. Add to the saucepan and cook, whisking, for 2 minutes, or until thickened. Serve over the pork.

Makes 4 servings

Per serving: *476 calories, 43 g protein, 46 g carbohydrates, 12 g fat, 110 mg cholesterol, 200 mg sodium, 4 g dietary fiber*

Diet Exchanges: *0 milk, 1 vegetable, 1 fruit, 1½ bread, 4½ meat, 1 fat*

Kitchen Tip

Serve this impressive pork dinner with a wild rice pilaf.

Herb-Crusted Leg of Lamb

167 Calories

MARINADE AND LAMB

⅔ cup fat-free beef broth

½ cup dry vermouth

¼ cup balsamic vinegar

1 tablespoon chopped fresh rosemary

2 cloves garlic, minced

1 teaspoon salt

¼ teaspoon black pepper

1 boneless leg of lamb (4 pounds), butterflied and trimmed of all visible fat

GARLIC-HERB PASTE

1 bulb garlic

2 tablespoons chopped fresh rosemary

2 tablespoons chopped fresh oregano

½ teaspoon black pepper

1 tablespoon olive oil

To make the marinade and lamb:

In a 13" × 9" baking dish, combine the broth, vermouth, vinegar, rosemary, garlic, salt, and pepper. Place the lamb in the marinade and turn to coat. Cover, refrigerate, and marinate for at least 4 hours or overnight, turning the lamb occasionally.

To make the garlic-herb paste:

Preheat the oven to 400°F.

Slice ¼" off the top of the garlic bulb and discard. Set the bulb on a large piece of foil, sprinkle with 1 tablespoon water, and wrap loosely. Bake for 25 minutes, or until very soft. Remove from the oven, unwrap, and let cool. Squeeze the garlic into a small bowl and dis-

card the papery skins. Using a fork, mash the garlic to a paste. Add the rosemary, oregano, parsley, pepper, and oil and mix well.

Increase the oven temperature to 450°F.

Remove the lamb from the marinade; roll it up and tie together with kitchen string. Pour the marinade into a small bowl; refrigerate until needed.

Place the lamb on a rack in a small roasting pan and roast for 15 minutes. Reduce the heat to 350°F and roast for 30 minutes.

Remove the lamb from the oven and slather with the garlic-herb paste. Rotate the pan and return to the oven. Roast for 40 to 50 minutes, or until a thermometer inserted in the thickest part registers 145°F for medium-rare. (For medium-well, continue to roast, checking every 5 minutes, until the temperature registers 160°F.) Place the lamb on a cutting board, cover lightly with foil, and let stand for 15 minutes before removing string and carving.

Pour off and discard any fat from the roasting pan. Add the reserved marinade to the pan. Place over medium-high heat and bring to a boil, scraping the browned bits from the bottom of the pan. Boil gently until the liquid is reduced by one-half.

Makes 16 servings

Per serving: *167 calories, 22 g protein, 3 g carbohydrates, 6 g fat, 65 mg cholesterol, 55 mg sodium, 1 g dietary fiber*

Diet Exchanges: *0 milk, 0 vegetable, 0 fruit, 0 bread, 3 meat, 1 fat*

Chicken Parmesan

328 Calories

—Rose Nicolini, Lighthouse Point, Florida

"Low in calories and very tasty, this dish won't make you feel deprived, so it is easy to stay on track with your diet."

¼ cup liquid egg substitute

1 cup Italian or whole wheat bread crumbs

½ cup (2 ounces) grated Parmesan cheese

2 tablespoons chopped parsley

2–3 cloves garlic, minced

4 boneless skinless chicken breast halves, pounded to ½" thickness

1 cup tomato sauce

1 cup (4 ounces) shredded reduced-fat mozzarella cheese

Preheat the oven to 375°F. Coat a baking sheet with cooking spray.

Place the egg substitute in a shallow dish. In another shallow dish, combine the bread crumbs, Parmesan, parsley, and garlic. Dip the chicken in the egg substitute, then dredge in the bread-crumb mixture. Place the chicken on the prepared baking sheet.

Bake for 10 minutes. Place ¼ cup of the tomato sauce over each chicken breast half and top each with ¼ cup of the mozzarella. Bake for 20 minutes, or until a thermometer inserted in the thickest portion registers 160°F and the juices run clear and the cheese is melted.

Makes 4 servings

Per serving: *328 calories, 53 g protein, 7 g carbohydrates, 10 g fat, 120 mg cholesterol, 861 mg sodium, 1 g dietary fiber*

Diet Exchanges: *0 milk, 1 vegetable, 0 fruit, 0 bread, 7 meat, ½ fat*

REJOICE, FAST-FOOD FANS!

You know the advantage of fast food: It's quick and it tastes good. But there are ways to get the "fast" without the fat.

Many burger places offer grilled chicken sandwiches and salad bars. If fried chicken is your weakness, pick off the breading to strip calories while retaining the flavor. Overall, sub shops are a pretty safe bet—if you go easy on the mayo.

Your grocery store is a great place to pick up healthy convenience foods such as reduced-fat hot dogs, low-fat frozen dinners, and stir-fry ensembles for quick meals at home. But when you just can't shake the craving, it's perfectly fine to hit your local hot dog stand or burger joint once in a while—just mini-size your meal.

It Worked for Us!

Ann and Butch Painter

Making the switch from french fries to salad was a lot easier for Ann and Butch Painter than it might have been—because they did it together.

"Our children had finally all left home for college. That was when we looked at each other and decided that if we wanted to enjoy the rest of our lives together healthily, it was time to lose weight.

"Butch is a truck driver and is required to have an annual physical. Last year, we both went to the doctor together and announced our plans. The doctor was thrilled! As it turns out, he also had lost a substantial amount of weight in the past, and so he had a lot of advice to offer. He talked to us about the psychological reasons for overeating, and suggested a month of journaling about when and why we were hungry.

"Being accountable for our weight loss was what really did the trick. Once we left the doctor's office after that first visit, we had an appointment to go back in 3 weeks. We didn't want to be failures—to disappoint both ourselves and the doctor—so we stuck to our plan. We continued to have follow-up visits at regular intervals—6 weeks, then 3 months, and then 6 months. Knowing we had those standing appointments kept us working steadily toward our goals.

"Doing this as a team also made a big difference. We do the grocery shopping together and pick out fresh fruits and vegetables that we know we'll both eat. Plus, we read labels on any other food items we buy. While we certainly don't feel deprived (especially since we discovered fat-free chocolate pudding), we're lucky we don't have any kids at home to complain about the lack of junk food in the house!

"As for exercise, Butch gets quite a workout through his job, and I use aerobics videotapes at home. But we also try to walk together whenever we can. Spending this kind of time together is a special benefit of doing this as a couple. But probably the greatest good all this weight loss has done is improve our health. Butch has a lot fewer problems with his knees and back, and I feel better, too—I have a lot more energy and much less fatigue."

Baked Chicken and Vegetable Couscous

550 Calories

CHICKEN AND MARINADE

- 1 lemon
- 1 cup fat-free plain yogurt
- 1 tablespoon grated fresh ginger
- 2 cloves garlic, minced
- 1½ teaspoons turmeric
- 1 teaspoon ground cumin
- ¼ teaspoon black pepper
- 4 bone-in skinless chicken breast halves

VEGETABLES AND COUSCOUS

- 4 carrots, cut into 1" pieces
- 4 parsnips, cut into 1" pieces
- 1 red onion, cut into 1" pieces
- 1 butternut squash, peeled and cubed
  Salt and black pepper
- 1½ cups fat-free chicken broth
- ½ box (5 ounces) couscous

To make the chicken and marinade:

Grate the rind from the lemon into a shallow 3-quart baking dish. Cut the lemon in half and squeeze the juice into the baking dish. Discard the lemon. Stir in the yogurt, ginger, garlic, turmeric, cumin, and pepper. Add the chicken and turn to coat. Cover and refrigerate for at least 4 hours or up to 12 hours; turn at least once while marinating.

To make the vegetables and couscous:

Preheat the oven to 400°F. Coat 2 baking sheets with cooking spray.

Place the carrots, parsnips, onion, and squash on the prepared baking sheets and season with salt and pepper. Bake for 30 minutes, or until almost tender. Remove from the oven. Reduce the temperature to 375°F.

Uncover the chicken and add the broth to the baking dish. Cover the chicken loosely with foil and bake for 25 minutes, basting occasionally with the marinade. Remove the foil, turn the chicken over, and add the vegetables. Bake for 12 minutes, or until a thermometer inserted in the thickest portion of the chicken registers 170°F and the juices run clear.

Meanwhile, prepare the couscous according to package directions. Serve with the chicken and vegetables.

Makes 4 servings

Per serving: *550 calories, 44 g protein, 89 g carbohydrates, 3 g fat, 75 mg cholesterol, 240 mg sodium, 15 g dietary fiber*

Diet Exchanges: *½ milk, 4 vegetable, 0 fruit, 3½ bread, 4½ meat, 0 fat*

Kitchen Tip

To peel and cube winter squash, cut it in half and remove the seeds. Cut the halves into 2" sections and, using a sharp knife, cut the flesh away from the skin.

Peanut Chicken

—**Christine Carro, East Greenbush, New York**

" After reading the oatmeal–peanut butter cookie recipe in Prevention's Mailbag, I decided to try other ways of enjoying my PB and losing weight. This is a great change of pace from roasted, baked, and grilled chicken breasts. "

4 boneless, skinless chicken breast halves
¼ teaspoon salt
2 tablespoons creamy peanut butter
1 teaspoon reduced-sodium soy sauce
⅛–¼ cup water
1 teaspoon sesame seeds

Preheat the oven to 350°F. Coat a 13" × 9" baking pan with cooking spray.

Season the chicken with the salt and place in the prepared baking pan.

In a small microwaveable bowl, combine the peanut butter, soy sauce, and ⅛ cup of the water and microwave on high power for 30 seconds. Stir until smooth and well-mixed. Add up to ¼ cup more water for a thinner sauce. Drizzle over the chicken and sprinkle with the sesame seeds.

Bake for 25 minutes, or until a thermometer inserted in the thickest portion registers 160°F and the juices run clear.

Makes 4 servings

Per serving: *240 calories, 42 g protein, 2 g carbohydrates, 7 fat, 100 mg cholesterol, 338 mg sodium, 1 g dietary fiber*

Diet Exchanges: *0 milk, 0 vegetable, 0 fruit, 0 bread, 6 meat, 1 fat*

BOOST YOUR DIETING WILLPOWER

Research shows that individuals who exercise at least 3 hours a week tend to eat a more balanced diet. Here's why.

You'll think twice before over-indulging because you won't want to negate all the calories you just exercised off. For example, a large serving of french fries will undo more than 5 miles of walking.

You won't have to cut so many calories from your diet and risk feeling deprived. Instead of eating 500 fewer calories a day to lose a pound a week, you'll only have to cut back by 200 calories a day if you're exercising off the other 300.

Exercise feels better than eating. Snacking on a heavy dessert or a whole bag of chips can make you feel sluggish. Opt instead for an invigorating walk—you'll love the way it makes you feel.

Chicken and Black Beans

446 Calories

—Meg Bruhn, Gillespie, Illinois

" This is a quick dinner I can fix for the family. I love to experiment with food, and this is one I am very proud of. I prefer the Crock-Pot method (see tip) because it's ready when I walk in the door. It's healthy, tasty, filling, and easy! "

1 cup brown rice
8 ounces sliced button mushrooms
1 can (14–19 ounces) black beans, drained
1 can (14½ ounces) diced tomatoes
1 onion, chopped
4 boneless, skinless chicken breast halves
¼ teaspoon salt
¼ teaspoon black pepper

Preheat the oven to 350°F. Coat a 13" × 9" baking dish with cooking spray.

Prepare the rice according to package directions.

Meanwhile, combine the mushrooms, beans, tomatoes (with juice), and onion in the prepared baking dish. Place the chicken on top and sprinkle with the salt and pepper. Bake for 45 minutes, or until a thermometer inserted in the thickest portion registers 160°F and the juices run clear. Serve over the rice.

Makes 4 servings

Per serving: *446 calories, 50 g protein, 56 g carbohydrates, 4 g fat, 99 mg cholesterol, 696 mg sodium, 8 g dietary fiber*

Diet Exchanges: *0 milk, 1 vegetable, 0 fruit, 3 bread, 5½ meat, 0 fat*

Kitchen Tip

To prepare this dish in a slow cooker, combine all the ingredients except the rice in a slow cooker and cook on the low heat setting for 6 to 8 hours. You can prepare the rice the night before and simply heat it up at dinnertime.

Sweet-and-Spicy Stuffed Chicken

348 Calories

- 2 tablespoons olive or vegetable oil
- 4 ounces mushrooms, finely chopped
- 1 scallion, finely chopped
- 2 cups cornbread-, herb-, or chicken-seasoned stuffing mix
- 8 boneless, skinless chicken breast halves, pounded thin, or 8 boneless, skinless chicken breast cutlets
- 1 egg, beaten
- ½ cup seasoned bread crumbs
- ½ small red bell pepper, finely chopped
- ½ cup apple jelly
- 1 tablespoon Dijon mustard
- ¼ teaspoon hot-pepper sauce

Preheat the oven to 350°F. Coat a 13" × 9" baking pan with cooking spray.

Heat 1 tablespoon of the oil in a large skillet over medium-high heat. Add the mushrooms and cook, stirring occasionally, for 4 minutes. Add the scallion and cook for 1 minute. Remove from the heat.

Prepare the stuffing mix according to package directions. Stir in the mushroom mixture. Evenly divide the mixture among the chicken breast halves, patting the stuffing evenly over the chicken. Roll the chicken around the stuffing and secure with wooden picks.

Place the egg and bread crumbs in separate shallow bowls. Roll the stuffed chicken in the egg and then in the bread crumbs. Place in the prepared baking pan. Bake for 25 minutes, or until the chicken is no longer pink. Do not turn off the oven.

Meanwhile, in the same skillet, heat the remaining 1 tablespoon oil over medium-high heat. Add the bell pepper and cook, stirring occasionally, for 4 minutes. Stir in the jelly, mustard, and hot-pepper sauce and cook for 2 minutes. Spoon the sauce evenly over the rolls and bake for 5 minutes longer. Slice the chicken rolls and serve.

Makes 8 servings

Per serving: *348 calories, 31 g protein, 31 g carbohydrates, 11 g fat, 100 mg cholesterol, 550 mg sodium, 2 g dietary fiber*

Diet Exchanges: *0 milk, 0 vegetable, 0 fruit, 2 bread, 4 meat, 1½ fat*

Kitchen Tip

Rice pilaf makes a nice accompaniment to these chicken rolls.

Scallops in Citrus Marinade

—Ilene Goldberg, Newington, Connecticut

"You can use this marinade for boneless, skinless chicken breast and then grill it. I also use it on fresh steamed veggies—everything from broccoli to asparagus to baby spinach."

1 cup orange juice

½ cup water

¼ cup lime juice

2 tablespoons olive oil

¼ cup packed light brown sugar

1 teaspoon ground ginger

1 teaspoon minced garlic

½ teaspoon dried Italian seasoning

¼ teaspoon salt

⅛ teaspoon ground black pepper

1½ pounds fresh or thawed frozen sea scallops, rinsed

In a resealable plastic bag, combine the orange juice, water, lime juice, oil, brown sugar, ginger, garlic, Italian seasoning, salt, and pepper. Add the scallops, seal the bag, and marinate in the refrigerator for no more than 1 hour.

Preheat the oven to 400°F.

Place the scallops and marinade in a single layer in an 8" × 8" baking dish. Bake for 20 minutes, or until the scallops are opaque.

Makes 4 servings

Per serving: *252 calories, 29 g protein, 14 g carbohydrates, 8 g fat, 55 mg cholesterol, 430 mg sodium, 0 g dietary fiber*

Diet Exchanges: *0 milk, 0 vegetable, ½ fruit, ½ bread, 4 meat, 1½ fat*

Kitchen Tip

Don't let a drop of this delicious marinade go to waste! Toss the scallops and marinade with 8 ounces of your favorite strand pasta, like linguine or fettuccine. The marinade will coat the pasta with wonderful citrusy flavor.

It Worked for Me!

Jennifer Jensen

VITAL STATS

Weight lost: 25 pounds

Time to goal: 2 years

Unique secret to success: Aim high—shooting for nine servings of fruits and vegetables daily means you'll get at least six; planning to exercise every day helps you get in a minimum of three workouts a week

*R*eading articles and books about people who succeeded at weight loss really got Jennifer fired up to work toward her own goal.

"For me, losing weight came about as a lifestyle change rather than a strict 'diet.' I started by joining a Weight Watchers group back in May of 2000, and I have been going semifaithfully ever since.

"I drink a lot of water and find that it's a powerful tool. I have a 20-ounce bottle that I just keep on refilling—a couple in the morning and a couple in the afternoon. And I can feel the effect. In fact, if I don't drink enough water, I tend to feel sluggish and might wind up turning to food for energy. If I am on track with my water, I'm on track with my weight loss.

"I also try to prevent getting too hungry, especially at certain times of day when that becomes dangerous. After work, before starting to prepare dinner, I make sure to sit down and have a little something to eat—say, an apple or a couple of graham crackers.

Otherwise, I wind up snacking while I'm cooking, and basically eat two dinners.

"When you're trying to lose weight, fruits and vegetables are the way to go. I picture my plate at every meal, and make sure at least half is produce—that's a no-brainer technique. Also, I aim really high. My goal is to eat nine servings of fruits and vegetables a day. That way, even if I don't actually eat that much, I get at least the six you're supposed to strive for. Another tip: It's easiest for me to wash and cut them right away, as soon as I get home from the grocery store. Then, when I want something to eat, they are easy to grab.

"I aim high with exercise, too. I make plans to walk on my treadmill every single day. Of course, I can't always keep that promise, but even if I miss 3 days I'm still walking on 4 days, which isn't too bad. It's also helpful to get on that treadmill as soon as I get home in the evening. If I wait too long, or get involved in some other project like laundry or supper, I just won't do it. Even when that happens, I try not to get angry with myself. I just set my sights on the next day."

Crispy Baked Catfish

244 Calories

—Marla Holbrook, Montgomery, Alabama

"This recipe added good-for-me fish to my diet, cooked in a way that's tasty and low-calorie."

½ **cup liquid egg substitute**
1 **cup crushed low-fat crackers**
¼ **cup (1 ounce) grated Parmesan cheese**
1 **tablespoon crab boil seasoning**
4 **catfish fillets (5 ounces each)**

Preheat the oven to 425°F. Coat a 13" × 9" baking dish with cooking spray.

Place the egg substitute in a shallow bowl. In another shallow bowl, combine the crackers, cheese, and crab boil seasoning. Dip the fillets in the egg substitute, then in the cracker mixture, pressing gently to adhere. Place in the prepared baking dish. Coat the fish with cooking spray.

Bake for 15 minutes, or until the fish flakes easily.

Makes 4 servings

Per serving: *244 calories, 32 g protein, 13 g carbohydrates, 6 g fat, 70 mg cholesterol, 1,050 mg sodium, 1 g dietary fiber*

Diet Exchanges: *0 milk, 0 vegetable, 0 fruit, 1 bread, 1 meat, ½ fat*

SHORT-CIRCUIT A BINGE

You've devoured an entire bag of potato chips and dip—and now you're reaching for the ice cream. Hang on! "Learning from your mistakes is an important step to long-term weight-loss success," says Lee Kern, clinical director at Structure House, a weight-loss center in Durham, North Carolina. Here's how to regain control.

1. **Stop right there.** Throw out the cookie box, brush your teeth, and remind yourself that 400 calories is a lot easier to deal with than the 4,000 you might have consumed if you'd kept right on eating.
2. **Calm down.** Take a deep breath and distance yourself from the incident: Clean out a closet, take a shower, go for a walk.
3. **Renew your commitment.** Forgive yourself and get right back on your healthy eating plan.
4. **Reflect on the reasons.** Have you been breaking from your routine, staying up late, and skipping breakfast, so you're starting the day tired and hungry? Do you head for the drive-thru when you see fast-food commercials? Use this information to prevent future binges.
5. **Call a friend.** Talking through your experience right away provides tremendous emotional relief.

Sweet Maria's Salmon

—Michele Patsula, Calgary, Alberta

"This dish satisfies my sweet craving but with protein power!"

2 tablespoons balsamic vinegar
1 tablespoon olive oil
1 clove fresh garlic, minced
1 tablespoon packed brown sugar
¼ teaspoon dried rosemary
¼ teaspoon chopped fresh dill
¼ teaspoon black pepper
4 salmon fillets (6 ounces each), skinned
½ teaspoon salt

Preheat the oven to 450°F. Line a baking sheet with foil.

In a small bowl, combine the vinegar, oil, garlic, brown sugar, rosemary, dill, and pepper. Place the salmon on the prepared baking sheet and brush with the vinegar mixture. Refrigerate for 30 minutes.

Remove from the refrigerator and sprinkle with the salt. Roast for 15 minutes, or until the fish is opaque.

Makes 4 servings

Per serving: *361 calories, 34 g protein, 5 g carbohydrates, 22 g fat, 100 mg cholesterol, 390 mg sodium, 0 g dietary fiber*

Diet Exchanges: *0 milk, 0 vegetable, 0 fruit, ½ bread, 5 meat, 1 fat*

SECRETS OF WEIGHT-LOSS WINNERS

• Counting calories, using a smaller plate, and keeping a daily journal help me. So do drinking six to eight glasses of water a day and having a "diet" friend to talk to.

—Sally Dugan, Faucett, Missouri

• The DietPower software program taught me how to monitor my food intake. I learned about calories as well as how to balance fat, fiber, protein, cholesterol, and vitamins. It's easy to log exactly what I eat and plan my meals.

—Susan Glazer, Langhorne, Pennsylvania

• Clean out your fridge and cabinets of all the no-nos. Stock up on all the wonderful healthy things that you *can* eat. And invest in a good light and quick cookbook.

—Loise DiPalma, Wallingford, Connecticut

Salmon with White Beans and Watercress

286 Calories

4 salmon fillets (4 ounces each)
  Salt and black pepper
2 tablespoons water
2 cloves garlic, minced
1 can (14–19 ounces) cannellini beans, rinsed and drained
4 plum tomatoes, chopped
½ cup fat-free chicken broth
1 bunch watercress, rinsed and coarsely chopped
¼ cup chopped Italian parsley

Coat a broiler-pan rack with cooking spray. Preheat the broiler.

Season the fillets with salt and pepper and place on the prepared rack. Broil 4" from the heat for 3 minutes per side, or until just opaque.

Meanwhile, bring the water to a boil in a large nonstick skillet over medium-high heat. Add the garlic and stir for 1 minute. Add the beans, tomatoes, and broth and cook, stirring occasionally, for 3 minutes, or until heated through. Add the watercress and parsley and cook for 30 seconds, or until the watercress begins to wilt. Season with salt and pepper. Serve with the salmon.

Makes 4 servings

Per serving: *286 calories, 29 g protein, 17 g carbohydrates, 13 g fat, 65 mg cholesterol, 410 mg sodium, 5 g dietary fiber*

Diet Exchanges: *0 milk, 1/2 vegetable, 0 fruit, ½ bread, 3½ meat, ½ fat*

Sole in Parchment

211 Calories

3 tablespoons fat-free mayonnaise

2 tablespoons minced shallots

1 tablespoon Dijon mustard

1 tablespoon lemon juice

1 clove garlic, minced

½ teaspoon dried dill

4 sole fillets (6 ounces each)

4 plum tomatoes, sliced lengthwise

1 zucchini, cut into matchsticks

1 yellow squash, cut into matchsticks

4 tablespoons white wine or nonalcoholic white wine

¼ teaspoon salt

¼ teaspoon black pepper

Preheat the oven to 450°F. In a small bowl, combine the mayonnaise, shallots, mustard, lemon juice, garlic, and dill.

Cut 4 pieces of parchment paper, each 14" long. For each packet, lay 1 piece of parchment on a work surface with a long edge facing you, like an open book. Place a fillet on one half of the parchment. Spread 1 tablespoon of the sauce over the fillet. Top with overlapping tomato slices, zucchini strips, and yellow squash strips. Pour 1 tablespoon of the wine over each fillet and season with the salt and pepper. Fold the parchment over the fillets so that the short edges come together (as if you were closing a book). Seal the packages by tightly rolling up and crimping each of the 3 open edges.

Place the packages on a baking sheet and lightly coat with cooking spray. Bake for 10 minutes, or until the packets are puffed and browned. Place on dinner plates and cut an X in the top of each package. Fold back the corners and serve.

Makes 4 servings

Per serving: *211 calories, 34 g protein, 9 g carbohydrates, 3 g fat, 85 mg cholesterol, 480 mg sodium, 2 g dietary fiber*

Diet Exchanges: *0 milk, 1 vegetable, 0 fruit, ½ bread, 4½ meat, ½ fat*

Kitchen Tip

The fish packets can be assembled and refrigerated for up to 8 hours before baking. You can remove the fish and vegetables from the parchment before serving, but the presentation will be less dramatic.

Hamburger Hot Dish

282 Calories

—Debbie Opdahl, Northwood, North Dakota

"We used to eat a lot of hot dishes, and this is my diet version of it. It is so easy to make and tastes good, too. It's much lower in calories than my original recipe."

½ **pound lean ground beef**
½ **cup (3 ounces) elbow macaroni**
1 **can (14½ ounces) stewed tomatoes**
1 **can (15¼ ounces) whole kernel corn**

Cook the beef in a medium nonstick skillet over medium-high heat for 5 minutes, or until no longer pink. Drain and return to the skillet.

Add the macaroni, tomatoes (with juice), and the liquid from the corn. Cook, stirring occasionally, for 10 minutes, or until the macaroni is al dente. Add the corn and heat through.

Makes 4 servings

Per serving: *282 calories, 17 g protein, 34 g carbohydrates, 6 g fat, 21 mg cholesterol, 562 mg sodium, 4 g dietary fiber*

Diet Exchanges: *0 milk, 2 vegetable, 0 fruit, 0 bread, 2 meat, 0 fat*

ATTENTION, MEAT LOVERS!

The key to losing weight while still eating the comfort foods you grew up with is learning how to prepare them with fewer calories. Start with smart choices: Lean cuts of red meat such as top round, sirloin, and London broil average 240 calories per 3-ounce serving.

(Their fattier cousins—prime rib, T-bone, and filet mignon—weigh in at 340 calories.) Then grill or sauté them in olive-oil spray instead of butter to cut calories even further. For variety, try pork tenderloin or tuna steak as hearty red-meat substitutes.

It Worked for Me!

Kelly Jens

VITAL STATS

Weight lost: 92 pounds

Time to goal: 10 months

Unique secret to success: Reinventing restaurant meals and using fast-food nutrition guides to make smarter choices when eating out

Kelly was a mother of two young children, but her weight kept her from joining in their energetic play. Changing her diet changed her life—as well as those of her children.

"The photograph on my family's 1997 Christmas card says it all. The frame is dominated by great big me—my husband and two children could barely squeeze into the shot. I looked at the picture and wondered to myself, 'How did I let this happen?'

"I knew how it happened. I'd gained 60 pounds from two pregnancies. But the fact was, I was afraid that as they grew up my children would be ashamed of me. I also worried about the kind of example I was setting for them.

"My family would eat out several times a week, and to me, the best restaurants were the ones with the largest portions. At home, I prepared rich, hearty meals. Weekend breakfasts would include bacon, eggs, hash browns, and biscuits with gravy. At lunchtime, spaghetti would be smothered in meat sauce. And dinner was often steak with potatoes slathered in sour cream and corn rolled in butter. Changing my diet really meant

learning how to control my portions and make better low-fat choices whenever I could.

"I read health magazines, clipped recipes, and bought a book filled with nutrition information on meals at popular restaurants such as Denny's, Olive Garden, and Arby's. I used the book and started keeping a food journal to help me limit my calories to less than 2,000 a day.

"My lifestyle changes didn't end at the dining table. I knew from what I'd read that I had to increase my activity level as well. But as a stay-at-home mom, my schedule really depends on my kids. Instead of trying to stick to a strict routine, I made a pact with myself to simply work some kind of exercise into each day.

"In the beginning I used a treadmill to walk on after the kids went to bed. When the weather got warmer, I walked outdoors in the mornings before anyone was awake. On days when I couldn't get out, I'd ride my exercise bike or pop a kickboxing tape in the VCR.

"My weight loss has paid off in pounds and inches—but also in laughter and energy. Before losing weight, I used to sit and just watch my children play. Now, I can join in and be a part of it all."

Chinese Pepper Steak

1½ cups white rice

2 teaspoons olive oil

1 large onion, thinly sliced

1 green bell pepper, thinly sliced

1 yellow bell pepper, thinly sliced

3 large plum tomatoes, thinly sliced

1 pound lean beef top round steak, trimmed of all visible fat and cut into ¼" × 2" strips

2 tablespoons cornstarch

1 teaspoon minced fresh ginger

1 clove garlic, minced

1 cup fat-free beef broth

1 cup water

¼ cup reduced-sodium soy sauce

Prepare the rice according to package directions.

Meanwhile, heat 1 teaspoon of the oil in a large nonstick skillet over medium heat. Add the onion and bell peppers and cook, stirring, for 5 minutes, or until softened. Add the tomatoes and cook, stirring, for 2 minutes. Place in a large bowl.

Heat the remaining 1 teaspoon oil in the skillet. Place the beef on a large plate and sprinkle with the cornstarch. Toss to coat. Add to the skillet and cook, stirring, for 2 minutes, or until lightly browned. Add the ginger and garlic. Stir for 1 minute, or until fragrant. Add the broth, water, and soy sauce to the skillet. With a wooden spoon, scrape up any browned bits from the bottom and sides of the skillet. Bring to a boil over medium-high heat. Reduce the heat to medium-low, cover, and simmer for 25 minutes, or until the beef is tender. Stir in the onion mixture and cook for 5 minutes, or until the vegetables are heated through. Add more water, if necessary, to thin the sauce. Serve over the rice.

Makes 4 servings

Per serving: *352 calories, 32 g protein, 32 g carbohydrates, 10 g fat, 65 mg cholesterol, 720 mg sodium, 4 g dietary fiber*

Diet Exchanges: *0 milk, 2 vegetable, 0 fruit, 1½ bread, 4 meat, 1½ fat*

Kitchen Tip

When choosing fresh ginger, look for extremely hard roots that easily snap into pieces. Store fresh ginger wrapped in a paper towel in a plastic bag in the refrigerator for up to 3 weeks. Or peel and place in a small container of white wine; refrigerate for up to 3 months. Use the wine to flavor soups, stews, and stir-fries.

Old-Fashioned Beef Stew

1 tablespoon olive oil

¼ cup unbleached all-purpose flour

¼ teaspoon black pepper

1½ pounds lean boneless beef round steak, trimmed of all visible fat and cut into 1" cubes

1 medium onion, chopped

2 cloves garlic, minced

1 teaspoon dried thyme

2 bay leaves

3 cups dry red wine or nonalcoholic red wine

¼ cup tomato paste

2 cans (14 ounces each) fat-free beef broth

1½ pounds baby red potatoes, quartered

20 baby carrots

16 baby pattypan squash, halved

1 pound shiitake mushrooms, thickly sliced

¼ cup chopped Italian parsley

Heat 1½ teaspoons of the oil in a Dutch oven over medium-high heat.

In a medium bowl, combine the flour and pepper. Working in batches, dredge the beef in the flour, place in the pot, and cook for 4 minutes, or until browned on all sides; do not overcrowd the pot. With a slotted spoon, remove the beef to a plate.

Add the remaining 1½ teaspoons oil to the pot. Reduce the heat to medium and add the onion, garlic, thyme, and bay leaves. Cook, stirring often, for 6 minutes, or until the onion is tender. Stir in the wine and tomato paste. With a wooden spoon, scrape up any browned bits from the bottom of the pot.

Add the broth and beef and bring to a boil. Partially cover and simmer for 1½ hours, or until the beef is tender.

Add the potatoes and carrots and simmer for 20 minutes. Add the squash, mushrooms, and parsley and simmer for 10 minutes, or until the vegetables are tender. Remove and discard the bay leaves before serving.

Makes 8 servings

Per serving: *330 calories, 22 g protein, 33 g carbohydrates, 6 g fat, 45 mg cholesterol, 130 mg sodium, 5 g dietary fiber*

Diet Exchanges: *0 milk, 2½ vegetable, 0 fruit, 1 bread, 2½ meat, 2½ fat*

Kitchen Tip

This stew keeps well in the refrigerator for up to 4 days. It also freezes well; store for no longer than 3 months. If needed, thin the sauce with a little water when reheating.

My Italian Chicken

—Susan Malbrough, Slidell, Louisiana

"You can also serve this dish over vegetable pasta. The longer you simmer it, the fuller the flavor will be."

1½ cups brown rice

3 large boneless, skinless chicken breast halves, cubed

16 ounces sliced mushrooms

10 Roma tomatoes, sliced

4 medium yellow squash, sliced

4 ribs celery, sliced

1 medium onion, finely chopped

1 large bell pepper, finely chopped

3 large cloves garlic, pressed

1 large can (28 ounces) crushed tomatoes

¼ cup chopped parsley

3 teaspoons Italian seasoning

1 teaspoon ground cumin

1 teaspoon salt

Prepare the rice according to package directions.

Meanwhile, heat a large pot coated with cooking spray over medium heat. Add the chicken and cook, stirring, for 3 minutes. Add the mushrooms, sliced tomatoes, squash, celery, onion, pepper, garlic, crushed tomatoes, parsley, Italian seasoning, cumin, and salt. Simmer for 20 minutes, or until the chicken is no longer pink and the vegetables are tender. Stir in the rice.

Makes 6 servings

Per serving: *430 calories, 36 g protein, 68 g carbohydrates, 3 g fat, 50 mg cholesterol, 860 mg sodium, 10 g dietary fiber*

Diet Exchanges: *0 milk, 2½ vegetable, 0 fruit, 3 bread, 3 meat, 0 fat*

Salsa Chicken

—**Mary Riney, Georgetown, Indiana**

"The amounts of salsa and spinach in this dish can vary, depending on your taste."

1 cup brown rice or 8 ounces whole wheat linguine

4 boneless, skinless chicken breast halves

1 bag (10 ounces) fresh spinach

¼ cup sliced green olives

1 jar (16 ounces) salsa

½ cup (2 ounces) shredded reduced-fat Mexican cheese

Prepare the rice or pasta according to package directions.

Meanwhile, heat a large nonstick skillet coated with cooking spray over medium heat. Add the chicken and cook, turning once, for 15 minutes, or until a thermometer inserted in the thickest portion registers 160°F and the juices run clear.

Push the chicken breasts to the sides of the skillet, leaving a space in the center. Add the spinach, olives, and salsa to the center of the skillet and stir to mix. Top with the chicken and sprinkle with the cheese. Cover and cook for 10 minutes, or until the spinach is wilted and the cheese is melted. Serve over the rice or linguine.

Makes 4 servings

Per serving: *440 calories, 50 g protein, 46 g carbohydrates, 6 g fat, 100 mg cholesterol, 860 mg sodium, 5 g dietary fiber*

Diet Exchanges: *0 milk, 2 vegetable, 0 fruit, 2½ bread, 6 meat, ½ fat*

SHOPPING SAVVY

Fiber-full Pasta

For added fiber at lunch or dinner, dig in to whole wheat pasta. Hodgson Mill makes a complete line of fiber-rich pasta, including fettuccine, spaghetti, bow-tie, lasagna, macaroni, penne, and angel hair. This pasta has three times the dietary fiber of refined flour pastas so you'll stay satisfied for hours. They're available at major grocery stores and at www.hodgsonmill.com.

Chicken Fettuccine Parmesan

—Cindy Rue, Lewisburg, Ohio

"My stepmom used to make this dish with a cream sauce, and I just dropped the sauce to make it low-calorie. It's also good cold."

8 ounces fettuccine

1 pound boneless, skinless chicken breast, cut into 1" cubes

1 red or green bell pepper, chopped

1 small onion, chopped

1 clove garlic, minced

½ teaspoon salt

¼ teaspoon black pepper

¼ cup (1 ounce) grated Parmesan cheese

Prepare the pasta according to package directions. Drain and place in a serving bowl.

Meanwhile, heat a large nonstick skillet coated with cooking spray over medium-high heat. Add the chicken, bell pepper, onion, and garlic and cook, stirring often, for 8 minutes, or until the chicken is no longer pink. Remove from the heat and add the salt and pepper. Add to the bowl with the fettuccine along with the cheese and toss to combine.

Makes 4 servings

Per serving: *319 calories, 35 g protein, 36 g carbohydrates, 4 g fat, 70 mg cholesterol, 559 mg sodium, 3 g dietary fiber*

Diet Exchanges: *0 milk, 1 vegetable, 0 fruit, 2 bread, 4 meat, 0 fat*

SECRETS OF WEIGHT-LOSS WINNERS

• When I have leftovers in portions too small for a whole meal, I put them on a frozen low-fat plain pizza. Almost any veggie works. I've even used beans. It's a great way to add hunger-squelching fiber.

—Dawn Biebl, Sidney, Montana

• I cut all milk protein from my diet. I've not only lost weight but gained energy. Now, I substitute unsweetened soy milk for cow's milk and use olive or canola oil for butter.

—Christine Ertell, Richmond, Virginia

5 STRATEGIES TO CONTROL YOUR APPETITE

Overeating—even healthy foods—may make it harder for your body to burn fat, suggests some preliminary research. It seems that chronically overindulging desensitizes fat cells to epinephrine, a hormone that is released during exercise and normally signals fat cells to empty their contents. So instead of exercising harder, you need to control your appetite to maximize your efforts. Here's how.

- Limit the calories you consume by having fewer choices. Serve a one-pot casserole such as beef and vegetable stew instead of steak, baked potatoes, and a buttered side dish.

- Enjoy dessert when eating out—without feeling guilty. But first, pass on the bread basket, skip the stuffed mushrooms, and bag half of your dinner.
- Keep a food diary. Write down exactly what and how much you'll have before sitting down—then stick to it.
- Curb late-night munchies by including a small amount of a satisfying fat at every meal: peanut butter, a pat of butter, or full-fat salad dressing.
- Leave something on your plate at each meal: the last bite of chicken or a forkful of stuffing. The calories you save will add up.

Easy Chicken with Black Beans and Rice

—Dee Tourville, Floral City, Florida

291 Calories

"This dish is easy to prepare, it tastes good, and it's low in fat. Remember, you can add more garlic and red pepper—I always do!"

1 cup white rice

½ pound boneless, skinless chicken breast, cubed

1 packet or cube (1 teaspoon) chicken bouillon

1 medium sweet onion, chopped

1 can (14–19 ounces) black beans, rinsed and drained

1 teaspoon garlic powder

¼–½ teaspoon ground red pepper

1½ cups water

Sea salt, to taste

Coarse black pepper, to taste

Prepare the rice according to package directions.

Heat a large skillet coated with cooking spray over medium heat. Place the chicken and bouillon in the skillet and cook, stirring frequently, for 4 minutes, or until no longer pink. Remove from the pan and set aside.

Recoat the skillet with cooking spray and reduce the heat to low. Add the onion and cook, stirring frequently, for 3 minutes, or until tender. Stir in the chicken, beans, rice, garlic powder, red pepper, and water and cook, stirring occasionally, for 5 minutes, or until heated through. Season with the salt and black pepper.

Makes 4 servings

Per serving: *291 calories, 20 g protein, 51 g carbohydrates, 1 g fat, 35 mg cholesterol, 860 mg sodium, 5 g dietary fiber*

Diet Exchanges: *0 milk, ½ vegetable, 0 fruit, 3 bread, 2 meat, 0 fat*

Chicken with Snow Peas

—Teena Perez, NY Mills, New York

"I use this recipe as part of an overall low-fat diet."

1½ cups white rice

6 boneless, skinless chicken breast halves

¼ teaspoon salt

¼ teaspoon white pepper

1 can (10¾ ounces) fat-free chicken broth

1 cup dry white wine

1 package (16 ounces) frozen snow peas

½ cup water

1 tablespoon cornstarch

Prepare the rice according to package directions.

Meanwhile, heat a large skillet coated with cooking spray over medium-high heat. Add the chicken and season with the salt and pepper. Cook, stirring occasionally, for 8 minutes, turn-

ing once. Remove the chicken from the pan.

Add the broth and wine to the pan and boil for 5 minutes. Add the reserved chicken and the snow peas and cook, stirring occasionally, for 4 minutes, or until a thermometer inserted in the thickest portion of the chicken registers 160°F and the juices run clear.

In a cup, combine the water and cornstarch. Add to the pan and stir until the sauce is thickened. Serve over the rice.

Makes 6 servings

Per serving: *364 calories, 33 g protein, 44 g carbohydrates, 2 g fat, 65 mg cholesterol, 210 mg sodium, 3 g dietary fiber*

Diet Exchanges: *0 milk, 0 vegetable, 0 fruit, 3 bread, 4 meat, ½ fat*

SECRETS OF WEIGHT-LOSS WINNERS

• To keep our spirits and dedication going, my husband and I allow ourselves Splurge Sunday. We go out to eat and have a great time, then it's back to healthier fare on Monday. We've lost over 70 pounds each.

—Ann Painter, Pittsburgh, Pennsylvania

• Every time I lost a pound, I gave myself a large colored paper clip. I

hooked together a chain and hung it on the refrigerator as a constant reminder of my progress and a way to focus on my goal.

—Carol Klabunde, Oshkosh, Wisconsin

• Wear black on your most bloated day. You'll look thinner, feel thinner, and be motivated to continue your program.

—Martha Whitestone, Bronx, New York

Thai Chicken Stir-Sizzle

315 Calories

PEANUT SAUCE

¾ cup water

¼ cup + 2 tablespoons creamy peanut butter

3 tablespoons soy sauce

2 tablespoons rice vinegar

¾ teaspoon red-pepper flakes

STIR-SIZZLE

6 ounces soba noodles or linguine

1 teaspoon toasted sesame oil

1 pound boneless, skinless chicken breast, sliced crosswise into ½" pieces

1 bunch scallions, sliced diagonally into 1" pieces

3 cloves garlic, minced

2 teaspoons grated fresh ginger

1 cup snow peas

1 red bell pepper, cut into thin strips

1 medium carrot, shredded

2 tablespoons chopped fresh cilantro

To make the peanut sauce:

In a blender, combine the water, peanut butter, soy sauce, and vinegar and process until smooth. Add the pepper flakes and set aside.

To make the stir-sizzle:

Prepare the noodles according to package directions. Drain and return to the pot.

Meanwhile, warm the oil in a large nonstick skillet over medium-high heat. Add the chicken and cook for 4 minutes, or until no longer pink. Add the scallions, garlic, and ginger and cook for 2 minutes, stirring often and being careful not to let the garlic burn. Add the snow peas, pepper, and carrot and cook for 2 minutes. Stir in the peanut sauce and pour over the noodles in the pot. Sprinkle with the cilantro and toss to coat. Place over heat for 2 minutes, or until heated through.

Makes 6 servings

Per serving: *315 calories, 27 g protein, 31 g carbohydrates, 10 g fat, 45 mg cholesterol, 870 mg sodium, 3 g dietary fiber*

Diet Exchanges: *0 milk, 1 vegetable, 0 fruit, 1½ bread, 3 meat, 1½ fat*

Chicken with Artichokes and Roasted Red Peppers

—Melissa Dumas, Lowell, Massachusetts

"I have been watching what I have been eating for a little over a year and lost 100 pounds—I feel great!"

3 tablespoons unbleached all-purpose flour

¼ teaspoon salt

¼ teaspoon black pepper

4 boneless, skinless chicken breast halves

12 ounces sliced mushrooms

1 shallot, chopped

1 package (10 ounces) artichoke hearts, thawed

½ cup sliced jarred roasted red peppers

½ cup white wine

1 cup fat-free chicken broth

In a shallow bowl, combine the flour, salt, and black pepper. Dredge the chicken in the flour mixture.

Heat a large skillet coated with cooking spray over medium heat. Add the chicken and cook, turning once, for 12 minutes, or until a thermometer inserted in the thickest portion registers 160°F and the juices run clear. Remove from the skillet and set aside.

Add the mushrooms and shallot to the skillet and cook for 3 minutes. Add the artichokes, roasted peppers, and wine and cook for 3 minutes. Add the broth and reserved chicken and bring to a boil. Reduce the heat to low and cook for 10 minutes longer, or until heated through.

Makes 4 servings

Per serving: *301 calories, 46 g protein, 16 g carbohydrates, 3 g fat, 100 mg cholesterol, 440 mg sodium, 5 g dietary fiber*

Diet Exchanges: *0 milk, 2 vegetable, ½ fruit, ½ bread, 6 meat, ½ fat*

Stir-Fry Spaghetti

—Lori Bailey, Joplin, Missouri

420 Calories

" My entire family enjoys this one—it's delicious! "

12 ounces spaghetti

2 tablespoons olive oil

1 clove garlic, minced

16 ounces smoked turkey sausage links, sliced

16 ounces frozen mixed vegetables, such as broccoli, red peppers, and mushrooms

2–3 teaspoons low-sodium teriyaki sauce

Prepare the pasta according to package directions. Drain and place in a serving bowl.

Meanwhile, heat the oil in a large skillet over medium heat. Add the garlic and cook for 2 minutes, or until fragrant. Add the sausage and cook, stirring occasionally, for 4 minutes, or until no longer pink. Add the vegetables and teriyaki sauce and cook, stirring frequently, for 10 minutes, or until the vegetables are tender. Add to the spaghetti in the bowl and toss to combine.

Makes 6 servings

Per serving: *420 calories, 21 g protein, 56 g carbohydrates, 13 g fat, 50 mg cholesterol, 760 mg sodium, 4 g dietary fiber*

Diet Exchanges: *0 milk, 0 vegetable, 0 fruit, 3 bread, 1½ meat, 1 fat*

MAKE YOUR DOCTOR A DIET BUDDY

Only 37 percent of severely overweight patients were given weight-control advice by their doctors, according to a study. Yet people whose doctors advise exercise are four times more likely to do it. So speak up! Here's how to get the quality care you deserve.

Be straight. Ask your doctor how he feels about working with someone overweight. If his reply is positive, you'll know you have a potential partner. If it's not, consider switching doctors.

Give details. Let your doctor know what you've been doing and where you need help.

Create an action plan. Request help prioritizing your efforts according to your health risks. If high cholesterol is a concern, you'll need to watch out for fatty foods. If you have joint pain, strength training may be your first step.

Ask for support in the form of a referral to the resource that will help you most, whether it's a dietitian, personal trainer, or emotional-eating workshop.

Follow up. Ask how often your doctor wants progress reports. Between office visits, ask if you can phone or e-mail weekly or monthly updates or questions.

Singapore Shrimp Noodles

334 Calories

6 ounces angel hair

1 teaspoon olive oil

1 bunch scallions, cut on the diagonal into 1" pieces

1 red bell pepper, cut into short strips

1 cup snow peas

2 cloves garlic, minced

1½ teaspoons grated fresh ginger

1 pound medium shrimp, peeled and de-veined

1 tablespoon curry powder

⅔ cup fat-free chicken broth

½ cup light coconut milk

¼ teaspoon harissa or chile paste

Prepare the pasta according to package directions. Drain and return to the pot.

Heat the oil in a large nonstick skillet over medium heat. Add the scallions, bell pepper, snow peas, garlic, and ginger and cook, stirring, for 1 minute. Add the shrimp and curry powder and cook for 2 minutes, or until the shrimp are opaque. Add the broth, coconut milk, and harissa or chile paste. Bring to a simmer.

Pour over the pasta in the pot and toss well. Cook, stirring constantly, over low heat for 2 minutes, or until the pasta has absorbed most of the sauce.

Makes 4 servings

Per serving: *334 calories, 31 g protein, 42 g carbohydrates, 4 g fat, 170 mg cholesterol, 230 mg sodium, 5 g dietary fiber*

Diet Exchanges: *0 milk, 1 vegetable, 0 fruit, 2½ bread, 3½ meat, ½ fat*

Kitchen Tip

Look for light coconut milk and harissa in the international section of your supermarket.

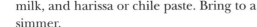

10 MINUTES TO WEIGHT CONTROL

If you eat slowly for the first 10 minutes of a meal, your brain will help you lose weight. High-tech images of the brains of 21 adults showed that 10 minutes after they started eating a meal, their brains turned off their appetite switches. At that point, the urge to continue eating lessens. So learn to pace yourself for 10 minutes instead of wolfing down your food. You'll find yourself satisfied with a smaller meal.

Mock Chow Mein

—Tina LaBrie, Estes Park, Colorado

"This makes a great one-dish supper for the whole family. I prefer using the soy pasta because it is higher in protein and fiber than regular pasta, and I think it tastes better, too."

8 ounces soy or whole wheat angel hair pasta, broken in half

1 small onion, chopped

1 teaspoon minced garlic

½ teaspoon grated ginger

3 medium carrots, cut into matchsticks

1 small head cabbage, shredded

2 cups cooked salad shrimp, cooked cubed chicken breast, or cooked cubed tofu

⅓ cup lite soy sauce

1 tablespoon lemon juice

Prepare the pasta according to package directions. Drain and place in a serving bowl.

Meanwhile, heat a large skillet coated with cooking spray over medium-high heat. Add the onion, garlic, and ginger and cook, stirring occasionally, for 3 minutes, or until the onion is translucent. Add the carrots and cabbage and cook, stirring frequently, for 5 minutes, or until tender.

Add the shrimp, chicken, or tofu, soy sauce, and lemon juice and cook for 3 minutes, or until heated through. Add to the pasta in the bowl and toss to combine.

Makes 6 servings

Per serving: *253 calories, 23 g protein, 39 g carbohydrates, 2 g fat, 145 mg cholesterol, 1,000 mg sodium, 9 g dietary fiber*

Diet Exchanges: *0 milk, 2 vegetable, 0 fruit, 1.5 bread, 2 meat, 0 fat*

Kitchen Tip

If your diet requires less sodium, be sure to use reduced-sodium soy sauce in this recipe. You can also reduce the amount of soy sauce.

Garlic-Seafood Pasta

—Angie Spano, Stockton, California

"This is not only light but it also tastes fantastic! It goes great with a dinner salad."

12 ounces linguine or fettuccine

2 tablespoons lite butter or margarine

6 cloves garlic, minced

1 pound medium shrimp, peeled and deveined

1 package (8 ounces) imitation lobster bites

2 tablespoons grated Parmesan cheese

Prepare the pasta according to package directions.

Meanwhile, melt the butter or margarine in a medium skillet over medium heat. Add the garlic and cook for 1 minute. Add the shrimp and lobster bites and cook, stirring frequently, for 4 minutes, or until the shrimp are opaque. Remove from the heat and keep warm.

Place the pasta in a large bowl and toss with the garlic butter and seafood. Sprinkle with the cheese.

Makes 6 servings

Per serving: *333 calories, 24 g protein, 48 g carbohydrates, 5 g fat, 107 mg cholesterol, 380 mg sodium, 1 g dietary fiber*

Diet Exchanges: *0 milk, 0 vegetable, 0 fruit, 0 bread, ½ meat, 0 fat*

Kitchen Tip

If you prefer a milder flavor, reduce the amount of garlic to 1 clove, or to taste.

SHOPPING SAVVY

Super Sauces

Flavor-intensive toppings from Wild Thymes are not packed in tomato or cream sauce or pureed like pestos.

They're chunky vegetables and herbs tightly packed in extra-virgin olive oil with no saturated fat, no added salt, no sugar, and no cholesterol. The two flavors—Wild Mushrooms, Leeks and Roasted Tomatoes and Sun Dried Tomatoes, Olives, Capers, and Rosemary—also go great on pizza, focaccia bread, sandwiches, and even salads. With only 35 calories per tablespoon, there's no guilt included! Available at specialty stores and online at www.wildthymes.com.

Pasta with Shrimp and Sun-Dried Tomato Pesto

338 Calories

PESTO

- ½ cup dry-packed sun-dried tomatoes
- 2 tablespoons chopped toasted walnuts
- 2 cloves garlic
- 1 can (14½ ounces) whole tomatoes, drained
- ½ cup chopped Italian parsley
- ¼ cup chopped fresh oregano or basil
- 1 tablespoon + 1½ teaspoons grated Parmesan cheese
- 2 teaspoons olive oil

PASTA AND SHRIMP

- 10 ounces angel hair pasta
- 1 teaspoon olive oil
- 1 onion, sliced
- 1 red or green bell pepper, sliced
- 1 pound large shrimp, peeled and deveined
- ½ teaspoon black pepper
- ¼ teaspoon salt

To make the pesto:

Place the sun-dried tomatoes in a small bowl, cover with hot water, and let soak for 10 minutes, or until softened. Drain and reserve the liquid.

Place the sun-dried tomatoes in a food processor or blender. Add the walnuts and garlic and process briefly to combine. Add the whole tomatoes, parsley, oregano or basil, cheese, and oil and process until smooth. Add just enough of the reserved tomato soaking liquid to form a paste; process until smooth.

To make the pasta and shrimp:

Prepare the pasta according to package directions. Drain and place in a serving bowl.

Meanwhile, heat the oil in a large nonstick skillet over medium heat. Add the onion and cook, stirring frequently, for 5 minutes, or until softened. Add the bell pepper and cook, stirring frequently, for 5 minutes, or until softened. Add the shrimp and cook, stirring, for 3 minutes, or until the shrimp are opaque. Sprinkle with the black pepper and salt. Place in the bowl with the pasta and top with the pesto. Toss well to combine.

Makes 6 servings

Per serving: *338 calories, 25 g protein, 46 g carbohydrates, 7 g fat, 117 mg cholesterol, 327 mg sodium, 4 g dietary fiber*

Diet Exchanges: *0 milk, 1½ vegetable, 0 fruit, 2½ bread, 2½ meat, 1 fat*

― Kitchen Tip ―

The pesto can be tightly covered and stored for up to 2 weeks in the refrigerator or up to 4 months in the freezer.

Crab Cakes with Roasted Pepper Sauce

S A U C E
- 2 roasted red peppers
- ½ cup fat-free mayonnaise
- Black pepper

C R A B C A K E S
- 1 teaspoon olive oil
- ½ small onion, finely chopped
- 1 rib celery, finely chopped
- 1 egg white
- 2 tablespoons chopped Italian parsley
- 2 tablespoons fat-free mayonnaise
- 1 tablespoon lemon juice
- 1½ teaspoons crab boil seasoning
- ½ teaspoon dry mustard
- ¼ teaspoon paprika
- 1 pound lump crabmeat
- 1 cup fresh bread crumbs

To make the sauce:

Puree the roasted peppers in a food processor or blender. Add the mayonnaise and black pepper and process briefly to combine.

To make the crab cakes:

Heat the oil in a medium nonstick skillet over medium-high heat. Add the onion and celery and cook for 5 minutes, or until soft. Place in a large bowl. Stir in the egg white, parsley, mayonnaise, lemon juice, crab boil seasoning, mustard, and paprika. Stir in the crabmeat and mix thoroughly. Form into 8 patties. Roll in the bread crumbs to coat completely.

Heat a large nonstick skillet coated with cooking spray over medium-high heat. Add the crab cakes and cook for 2 minutes; cover and cook for 1 minute longer, or until browned on the bottom. Coat the tops with cooking spray and turn over. Cook for 2 minutes, uncovered, or until golden brown. Serve with the sauce.

Makes 4 servings

Per serving: *210 calories, 26 g protein, 19 g carbohydrates, 4 g fat, 115 mg cholesterol, 650 mg sodium, 2 g dietary fiber*

Diet Exchanges: *0 milk, 1 vegetable, 0 fruit, 1 bread, 3½ meat, ½ fat*

─ *Kitchen Tip* ─
The sauce can be made a day in advance and stored, covered, in the refrigerator.

Easy Creamy Pink Salmon

—Andrea Heesch, Hastings, Minnesota

"This is a fantastic recipe that is rich and filling. It's great served with couscous and steamed green beans (which I top lightly with olive oil, salt, and lemon juice) on the side."

¾ cup + 1 tablespoon water
1 teaspoon chicken broth granules
1½ teaspoons white cooking wine
4 pink salmon fillets (about 1½ pounds)
1 tablespoon unbleached all-purpose flour
12 cherry tomatoes, halved
1 scallion, chopped

Heat ¾ cup of the water in a deep skillet over medium-high heat. Add the chicken broth granules and wine and bring to a boil. Place the salmon, skin side down, in the pan. Reduce the heat to medium, cover, and cook for 10 minutes, or until the fish is opaque. Remove the salmon from the pan and remove and discard the skin. Place the salmon on a serving platter.

Increase the heat to high and bring the broth mixture to a boil.

Meanwhile, in a small bowl, combine the flour and the remaining 1 tablespoon water. Gradually add to the broth mixture, being careful that lumps do not form. Add the tomatoes and cook for 2 minutes, or until thickened. Pour the sauce over the salmon and top with the scallion.

Makes 4 servings

Per serving: *220 calories, 35 g protein, 5 g carbohydrates, 6 g fat, 90 mg cholesterol, 500 mg sodium, 1 g dietary fiber*

Diet Exchanges: *0 milk, 1 vegetable, 0 fruit, 0 bread, 5 meat, 1 fat*

Kitchen Tip

For a different twist, try sprinkling the salmon with a light dusting of bread crumbs or reduced-fat shredded cheese just before covering the pan.

Poached Cod Stew

—Andrea Filak, Glenshaw, Pennsylvania

" This is a low-fat, healthy meal that I can eat almost every day.
The veggies can be changed for variety—try carrots, spinach, lima beans, or green beans. "

1½ cups brown rice

2 medium zucchini, sliced

2 medium onions, sliced

2 ribs celery, sliced

1 can (15 ounces) stewed tomatoes

1 bottle (8 ounces) clam juice

1 can (14–19 ounces) black beans or
  kidney beans, rinsed and drained

¼ teaspoon salt

¼ teaspoon black pepper

1 pound cod fillet
  Hot-pepper flakes, to taste

Prepare the rice according to package directions.

Meanwhile, in a large saucepan, bring the zucchini, onions, celery, tomatoes (with juice), and clam juice to a boil over medium-high heat. Reduce the heat to low, cover, and simmer for 15 minutes, or until the vegetables are tender. Stir in the beans, salt, and pepper. Place the cod on top of the vegetables. Cook for 10 minutes, or until the fish flakes easily. Serve the stew over the rice.

Makes 8 servings

Per serving: *240 calories, 17 g protein, 42 g carbohydrates, 2 g fat, 25 mg cholesterol, 500 mg sodium, 6 g dietary fiber*

Diet Exchanges: *0 milk, 1 vegetable, 0 fruit, 2 bread, 1½ meat, 0 fat*

Neptune's Bounty Bouillabaisse

415 Calories

1 tablespoon olive oil

2 bottles (8 ounces each) clam juice

12 ounces small red potatoes, quartered

2 leeks, thinly sliced

1 medium onion, chopped

5 cloves garlic, minced

1 can (28 ounces) chopped Italian plum tomatoes

1 pound halibut, cut into 2" cubes

8 ounces bay scallops

8 ounces large shrimp, peeled and deveined

2–3 tablespoons chopped fresh tarragon or basil

Salt and black pepper

Bring the oil and the clam juice to a boil in a large pot over medium-high heat. Add the potatoes, leeks, onion, and garlic and cook for 4 minutes, or until the onion is lightly browned. Add the tomatoes (with juice) and bring to a boil. Cook for 10 minutes.

Add the halibut, scallops, and shrimp. Cook for 5 minutes, or until the fish is opaque and flakes easily. Stir in the tarragon or basil and season to taste with salt and pepper.

Makes 4 servings

Per serving: *415 calories, 50 g protein, 37 g carbohydrates, 8 g fat, 145 mg cholesterol, 390 mg sodium, 6 g dietary fiber*

Diet Exchanges: *0 milk, 3½ vegetable, 0 fruit, 1 bread, 6½ meat, ½ fat*

Kitchen Tip

Serve delicious herbed toast with this stew. Place sliced French bread on a baking sheet, brush with a little olive oil, and sprinkle with marjoram, garlic powder, and grated Romano cheese. Bake for 15 minutes.

Super-Stuffed Potatoes

166 Calories

4 russet potatoes

1 tablespoon unbleached all-purpose flour

1/8 teaspoon ground nutmeg

Pinch + 1/4 teaspoon salt

1 cup + 2/3 cup 1% milk

1 cup (4 ounces) shredded low-fat Cheddar cheese

1 package (10 ounces) frozen chopped broccoli, thawed

3 strips turkey bacon, chopped and cooked until crisp

Preheat the oven to 425°F.

Pierce the potatoes several times with a fork. Place in the oven and bake for 1 hour, or until tender when pierced with a fork. Remove and leave the oven on.

Meanwhile, in a small saucepan, combine the flour, nutmeg, and the pinch of salt. Gradually whisk in 1 cup of the milk until the flour dissolves. Cook, stirring, over medium heat for 5 minutes, or until thickened. Remove from the heat. Stir in the cheese until smooth. Set aside.

Holding the potatoes with an oven mitt, cut in half lengthwise. Scoop the flesh out into a bowl, leaving a 1/4" shell. Place the shells on a baking sheet. Mash the flesh with a potato masher. Stir in the remaining 2/3 cup milk and 1/4 teaspoon salt until smooth. Spoon the potato mixture into the shells. Top with the broccoli, bacon, and cheese sauce. Bake for 10 minutes, or until heated through.

Makes 8 servings

Per serving: *166 calories, 11 g protein, 31 g carbohydrates, 2 g fat, 10 mg cholesterol, 230 mg sodium, 4 g dietary fiber*

Diet Exchanges: *0 milk, 1/2 vegetable, 0 fruit, 1 1/2 bread, 1/2 meat, 1/2 fat*

Potatoes Peperonata

145 Calories

1½ pounds small red potatoes, cut into wedges

  1 tablespoon olive oil

1½ onions, thinly sliced

  2 cloves garlic, minced

  4 red and/or green bell peppers, chopped

  1 can (28 ounces) chopped tomatoes, drained

  3 scallions, thinly sliced

¼ cup slivered kalamata olives

¼ cup chopped fresh basil

¼ cup balsamic vinegar

  2 tablespoons chopped Italian parsley

  1 teaspoon black pepper

¼ teaspoon salt

Preheat the oven to 400°F. Line a baking sheet with foil.

Place the potatoes on the prepared baking sheet. Drizzle with 1½ teaspoons of the oil and toss to coat. Roast for 40 to 45 minutes, or until browned. Place in a large bowl.

Heat the remaining 1½ teaspoons oil in a large nonstick skillet over medium heat. Add the onions and garlic and cook, stirring, for 5 minutes. Add the bell peppers and cook, stirring, for 3 minutes, or until the vegetables are softened. Add the tomatoes and cook for 2 minutes, or until heated through.

Place in the bowl with the potatoes. Add the scallions, olives, basil, vinegar, parsley, black pepper, and salt. Toss to combine.

Cover and refrigerate for at least 3 hours before serving.

Makes 8 servings

Per serving: *145 calories, 5 g protein, 29 g carbohydrates, 4 g fat, 0 mg cholesterol, 180 mg sodium, 5 g dietary fiber*

Diet Exchanges: *0 milk, 2 vegetable, 0 fruit, ½ bread, 0 meat, ½ fat*

French Fries

—Peggy Laplante, Claremont, New Hampshire

"Lowering my fat intake took some thinking on my part. This idea worked for me. The french fries taste great. I don't have to worry about all that extra fat and grease."

6 potatoes, scrubbed and cut into ¼"-thick sticks
½ teaspoon salt
¼ teaspoon black pepper

Preheat the oven to 450°F. Coat 2 baking sheets with cooking spray.

Place the potatoes on the prepared baking sheets in a single layer and coat with cooking spray. Sprinkle with the salt and pepper.

Bake for 30 minutes, turning once, or until golden and tender. Serve immediately.

Makes 4 servings

Per serving: *150 calories, 6 g protein, 39 g carbohydrates, 0 g fat, 0 mg cholesterol, 290 mg sodium, 5 g dietary fiber*

Diet Exchanges: *0 milk, 0 vegetable, 0 fruit, 2 bread, 0 meat, 0 fat*

Sweet Potato Fries

—Debra Whitfield, Crowley, Texas

"My whole family loves these fries, even the kid that hates sweet potatoes! I like to make them because they are a good source of fiber and beta-carotene and are filling as well. I am a vegetarian, so I make them regularly and have a feast with them!"

4 sweet potatoes, peeled and cut into ¼"-thick sticks
1 tablespoon extra-virgin olive oil
2 teaspoons jerk seasoning
½ teaspoon salt

Preheat the oven to 400°F. Coat 2 baking sheets with cooking spray.

Place the sweet potatoes on the prepared baking sheet. Drizzle with the oil and

sprinkle with the jerk seasoning and salt. Bake for 30 minutes, turning once, or until golden and tender. Serve immediately.

Makes 6 servings

Per serving: *107 calories, 1 g protein, 22 g carbohydrates, 2 g fat, 0 mg cholesterol, 224 mg sodium, 3 g dietary fiber*

Diet Exchanges: *0 milk, 0 vegetable, 0 fruit, 1 bread, 0 meat, 0 fat*

4 DIET TRICKS THAT WORK

When researchers put 300 overweight adults on two different diet plans, they discovered that the people who ate a variety of meals based on the USDA's dietary guidelines lost three times more weight by year's end than those following a diet focused on lowering fat. Here are a few rules to get you started, recommended by study author Judith S. Stern, R.D., Sc.D.

Eat a cookie. Participants stayed satisfied by enjoying a daily 100-calorie "bonus" serving such as salad dressing, butter, or even an occasional sweet.

Downsize your kitchenware. To keep portion sizes under control, grab a juice glass instead of a tall one, a salad plate instead of the oversize kind, and teaspoons instead of serving spoons for condiments and sauces.

Plan for the future. Create a 7-day menu and shop now, when you can make a week's worth of smart choices at once.

Have an orange a day. Participants added an extra fruit, vegetable, or low-fat dairy product to each of their meals. This is as simple as an orange at breakfast, yogurt at lunch, and a salad with dinner.

Curried Sweet Potatoes

220 Calories

—**Emily Nakai, Vancouver**

"This is excellent for a quick meal or snack. It's very satisfying and wonderfully flavorful, so it keeps you happy mentally and physically."

2 **medium sweet potatoes, halved lengthwise**
1 **cup fat-free plain yogurt**
1 **teaspoon curry powder**
1 **scallion, finely chopped**
1 **tablespoon honey**

Preheat the oven to 400°F. Coat a baking sheet with cooking spray.

Place the sweet potatoes, cut side down, on the prepared baking sheet and bake for 30 minutes, or until tender. When cool enough to handle, cut into cubes.

In a small bowl, combine the yogurt and curry powder. Spoon over the sweet potatoes. Sprinkle with the scallion and drizzle with the honey.

Makes 4 servings

Per serving: *220 calories, 7 g protein, 52 g carbo-hydrates, 0 g fat, 5 mg cholesterol, 115 mg sodium, 4 g dietary fiber*

Diet Exchanges: *½ milk, 0 vegetable, 0 fruit, 2 bread, 0 meat, 0 fat*

SHOPPING SAVVY

Add Splash to Vegetables

If you're looking for ways to perk up your vegetables, try one of Lucini's two artisan vinegars. The Pinot Grigio White Wine Vinegar is made from 100% Pinot Grigio grapes and aged in oak casks, and the Gran Riserva Balsamico is made from Trebbiano grapes and aged for 10 years in heirloom wood casks. Look for them in better supermarkets, or call 888-5-LUCINI to find a store near you.

Mock Mashed Potatoes

—Rose Nicolini, Lighthouse Point, Florida

"I love mashed potatoes, but they're fattening. I have fooled friends with this recipe. Try making it for Thanksgiving!"

1 bag (10 ounces) frozen cauliflower
½ cup fat-free milk
1 packet or cube (1 teaspoon) chicken bouillon
1 tablespoon butter or margarine
1 tablespoon horseradish sauce
½ cup (2 ounces) shredded reduced-fat mozzarella cheese

Place the cauliflower in a microwaveable bowl and microwave on high power for 8 minutes; drain.

In a food processor, combine the cauliflower, milk, bouillon, butter, and horseradish sauce until smooth. Place in the bowl and sprinkle with the cheese. Microwave on high power for 2 minutes, or until the cheese is melted.

Makes 4 servings

Per serving: *93 calories, 6 g protein, 6 g carbohydrates, 6 g fat, 16 mg cholesterol, 432 mg sodium, 2 g dietary fiber*

Diet Exchanges: *0 milk, 1 vegetable, 0 fruit, 0 bread, ½ meat, 1 fat*

Broccoli and Mushroom Sauté

—Liz Bello, New Hartford, New York

"Holidays are very hard for people trying not to consume too many unwanted calories. This dish accompanies every Thanksgiving and Christmas dinner, as well as Easter ham, and steak and chicken just off the grill. It's a year-round winning recipe!"

2 teaspoons butter or margarine
2 ribs celery, chopped
1 small onion, chopped
2 packages (16 ounces each) broccoli cuts
2 cans (4 ounces each) mushrooms, drained
1 package (8 ounces) reduced-fat cream cheese
1 can (10¾ ounces) fat-free cream of mushroom soup
¾ cup Italian-flavored bread crumbs

Preheat the oven to 350°F. Coat an 11" × 7" baking pan with cooking spray.

Melt the butter or margarine in a large nonstick skillet over medium-high heat. Add the celery and onion and cook, stirring frequently, for 5 minutes, or until the onion is translucent. Add the broccoli and mushrooms and cook, stirring frequently, for 5 minutes, or until tender. Add the cream cheese and soup and stir until creamy. Stir in ½ cup of the bread crumbs. Place in the prepared baking dish and top with the remaining ¼ cup bread crumbs.

Bake for 30 minutes, or until hot and bubbly.

Makes 8 servings

Per serving: *195 calories, 9 g protein, 20 g carbohydrates, 10 g fat, 20 mg cholesterol, 610 mg sodium, 5 g dietary fiber*

Diet Exchanges: *0 milk, 1½ vegetable, 0 fruit, 1 bread, ½ meat, 1½ fat*

Asparagus Medley

—Diana Entenmann, Okeana, Ohio

"This is a wonderful accompaniment for chicken or fish, is sinfully delicious, and it's low in calories and fat."

1 pound asparagus, ends trimmed and stems cut into bite-size pieces

8 ripe olives, sliced

2 plum tomatoes, finely chopped

½ red onion, finely chopped

1 clove garlic, minced

1 tablespoon olive oil

2 tablespoons crumbled feta cheese

Preheat the broiler.

Combine the asparagus, olives, tomatoes, onion, and garlic in a jelly-roll pan. Drizzle with the oil and toss to coat. Sprinkle with the cheese and broil for 8 minutes, or until lightly browned and tender-crisp.

Makes 4 servings

Per serving: *90 calories, 3 g protein, 8 g carbohydrates, 5 g fat, 5 mg cholesterol, 130 mg sodium, 3 g dietary fiber*

Diet Exchanges: *0 milk, 1½ vegetable, 0 fruit, 0 bread, 0 meat, 1 fat*

Stuffed Vidalia Onions

4 **Vidalia onions**
½ **teaspoon olive oil**
3 **medium zucchini, shredded**
3 **cloves garlic, minced**
1 **teaspoon dried thyme**
1 **teaspoon dried basil**
3 **tablespoons unseasoned dry bread crumbs**
1 **tablespoon + 1½ teaspoons chopped toasted pine nuts**
3 **tablespoons grated Parmesan cheese**
Salt and black pepper

Preheat the oven to 400°F. Line a baking sheet with foil.

Cut about ½" off the top of each onion. Slightly trim the bottoms so the onions stand upright. Place the onions, cut side up, on the baking sheet and coat with cooking spray. Bake for 1 hour, or until soft. Set aside for 15 minutes, or until cool enough to handle.

Reduce the oven temperature to 350°F.

Remove and discard the onion peels. With a spoon, scoop out the onion centers, leaving a ½" shell. Chop the centers and reserve 1 cup for the stuffing; save the remainder for another use.

Heat the oil in a large nonstick skillet over medium heat. Add the zucchini, garlic, thyme, basil, and chopped onion. Cook for 6 minutes, or until the zucchini is softened and most of the liquid has evaporated. Remove from the heat and stir in the bread crumbs, pine nuts, and cheese. Season to taste with the salt and pepper. Mix well. Divide the filling among the onion shells.

Coat the baking sheet with cooking spray. Place the onions on the baking sheet and bake for 20 minutes, or until golden.

Makes 4 servings

Per serving: *170 calories, 8 g protein, 29 g carbohydrates, 4 g fat, 5 mg cholesterol, 125 mg sodium, 7 g dietary fiber*

Diet Exchanges: *0 milk, 4½ vegetable, 0 fruit, ½ bread, ½ meat, ½ fat*

Kitchen Tip

The onions can be roasted a day in advance. Serve cold, at room temperature, or reheated in the microwave.

Super Succotash

—Margaret Garner, St. Louis

127 Calories

"This succotash is filling and nutritious, and it also makes a good lunch with a piece of hearty bread. It can be prepared ahead, stored in the fridge, and reheated. It will keep for at least 2 days."

½ cup frozen baby lima beans

2 tablespoons olive oil

1 small onion, chopped

½ red bell pepper, chopped

¼ teaspoon salt

¼ teaspoon black pepper

½ teaspoon garlic powder

½ cup corn kernels

¼ cup fat-free milk or plain soy milk, warmed

Bring 2 cups water to a boil in a medium saucepan over medium-high heat. Add the beans and cook for 15 minutes. Drain.

Meanwhile, heat the oil in a medium skillet over medium heat. Add the onion and bell pepper and cook, stirring frequently, for 4 minutes, or until tender-crisp. Sprinkle with the salt, black pepper, and garlic powder. Add the corn and heat through.

Add the beans and milk. Stir thoroughly and remove from the heat. Cover and let stand for 2 minutes before serving.

Makes 4 servings

Per serving: *127 calories, 3 g protein, 14 g carbohydrates, 7 g fat, 0 mg cholesterol, 209 mg sodium, 2 g dietary fiber*

Diet Exchanges: *0 milk, ½ vegetable, 0 fruit, ½ bread, 0 meat, 0 fat*

Orange-Ginger Glazed Carrots

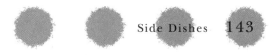

160 Calories

—Margaret Studer, Long Beach, California

"This goes well with any plain meat such as chicken breast or pork loin. And it makes a lovely accompaniment to homemade Chinese food. I like my carrots fairly crisp, but tender. If you like yours softer, you can steam them for about 10 minutes before you glaze them."

1 tablespoon butter or margarine
8 medium carrots, thinly sliced
½ teaspoon grated fresh ginger
¾ cup orange juice
¼ cup roasted almonds, slivered

Melt the butter or margarine in a medium skillet over medium heat. Add the carrots and cook, stirring occasionally, for 5 minutes. Add the ginger and cook for 2 minutes longer. Slowly add the orange juice and cook for 7 minutes, or until the carrots are tender and the juice begins to thicken. Increase the heat to medium-high and cook for 2 minutes, or until the liquid has been absorbed and the carrots have a brownish glaze. Serve sprinkled with the almonds.

Makes 4 servings

Per serving: *160 calories, 4 g protein, 21 g carbohydrates, 8 g fat, 8 mg cholesterol, 80 mg sodium, 6 g dietary fiber*

Diet Exchanges: *0 milk, 3 vegetable, ½ fruit, 0 bread, 0 meat, ½ fat*

Red Cabbage with a Twist

40 Calories

—Beryl McMaster, Melbourne, Florida

"This savory dish is low in calories and fat. You could even use it as a dessert!"

1 head red cabbage, chopped
1 red onion, chopped
3 tart apples, peeled and sliced
1 clove garlic, chopped
1½ cups chopped fresh cranberries
1 tablespoon + 1½ teaspoons packed brown sugar
1 tablespoon + 1½ teaspoons balsamic vinegar

Preheat the oven to 325°F.

Layer the cabbage, onion, apples, garlic, and cranberries in a 13" × 9" baking dish. Sprinkle with the brown sugar and vinegar. Cover and bake for 1½ hours, or until tender and cooked through. (The mixture will cook down by about half.) Stir before serving.

Makes 16 servings

Per serving: *40 calories, 1 g protein, 10 g carbohydrates, 0 g fat, 65 mg cholesterol, 210 mg sodium, 2 g dietary fiber*

Diet Exchanges: *0 milk, 1 vegetable, 0 fruit, 0 bread, 0 meat, 0 fat*

Lighter Fare

Sweet-and-Sour Cabbage Soup

118 Calories

—Elaine Brown, Charleston, South Carolina

"I am diabetic and have to watch my weight, sugar, and carbohydrates. This soup, made with a sugar substitute, is delicious and very low in fat and carbohydrates. It can be kept for 3 to 4 days, and it tastes better each day!"

½ pound lean ground beef

1 very large head cabbage, chopped

1 large onion, sliced

4 cups water

1 can (16 ounces) stewed tomatoes, chopped

1 can (8 ounces) tomato sauce

¼ cup packed brown sugar substitute or regular brown sugar

3 tablespoons lemon juice

1 tablespoon browning and seasoning sauce, such as Kitchen Bouquet

1 tablespoon Worcestershire sauce

½ teaspoon salt

¼ teaspoon black pepper

Heat a large pot coated with cooking spray over medium-high heat. Add the beef and cook, stirring frequently, for 5 minutes, or until no longer pink. Drain and return to the pot.

Add the cabbage, onion, water, tomatoes (with juice), tomato sauce, brown sugar, lemon juice, seasoning sauce, Worcestershire sauce, salt, and pepper and bring to a boil. Reduce the heat to low, cover, and simmer, stirring occasionally, for 2 to 2½ hours. If too sweet, add more lemon juice to taste; if too sour, add more brown sugar to taste.

Makes 10 servings

Per serving: *118 calories, 7 g protein, 19 g carbohydrates, 3 g fat, 0 mg cholesterol, 413 mg sodium, 4 g dietary fiber*

Diet Exchanges: *0 milk, 2½ vegetable, 0 fruit, ½ bread, 1 meat, 0 fat*

Souper-Fast Meal

332 Calories

—Carol Klabunde, Oshkosh, Wisconsin

"Because this soup is so easy to make and you can have so many variations depending on which type of vegetables you buy, my husband and I never tire of eating this except in the very hot summer weather. Use 'regular' vegetables or more exotic ones, depending on your tastes."

1½ **pounds ground chicken, turkey, or ground round**
1 **can (14¾ ounces) fat-free chicken broth**
1 **bag (16 ounces) frozen mixed vegetables**
1 **large onion, chopped**
1 **packet (1 ounce) onion soup mix**
½ **teaspoon salt**
¼ **teaspoon black pepper**

Heat a large pot coated with cooking spray over medium-high heat. Add the meat and cook, stirring frequently, for 8 minutes, or until no longer pink. Drain and return to the pot. Add the broth, mixed vegetables, onion, soup mix, salt, and pepper and bring to a boil. Reduce the heat to low, cover, and simmer for 10 minutes, or until the vegetables are tender.

Makes 4 servings

Per serving: *332 calories, 48 g protein, 23 g carbohydrates, 5 g fat, 119 mg cholesterol, 820 mg sodium, 6 g dietary fiber*

Diet Exchanges: *0 milk, 1 vegetable, 0 fruit, 1 bread, 6 meat, ½ fat*

SNACK ON SOUP

Having soup as an appetizer will help fill you up so you naturally eat less, and now it seems that a bowl between meals is better than other snacks at controlling your hunger.

When 24 women ate three different snacks that contained the same ingredients and calories—chicken rice casserole, the casserole with a glass of water, or a soup made with the casserole and water—the soup curbed their appetite the best. They reported less hunger and ate 80 fewer calories at a meal 2 hours later.

Part of the satisfaction you get from having broth-based soup is that you can eat a large portion while still sparing calories. So for a fast and filling snack, keep a 100-calorie cup of instant beef noodle or vegetable soup in your briefcase. During warm weather, try chilled soups such as strawberry and gazpacho.

California Chicken Soup

—Joan Grube, Alexandria, Ohio

"Soup is a dieter's friend—it's filling and healthful. This recipe can be prepared ahead of time and tastes even better when reheated. Serve with Italian bread."

3 cans (14¾ ounces each) fat-free chicken broth

2 cups water

1 pound cooked cubed chicken breast

2 medium carrots, chopped

1 small onion, chopped

1¾ teaspoons lemon pepper

1 teaspoon dried oregano

1 package (9 ounces) cheese tortellini

2 stalks broccoli, cut into florets (2 cups)

Freshly grated Parmesan cheese (optional)

In a large pot over medium-high heat, combine the broth, water, chicken, carrots, onion, lemon pepper, and oregano and bring to a boil. Add the tortellini. Reduce the heat to low and simmer for 25 minutes. Add the broccoli and cook for 5 minutes, or until the broccoli and tortellini are tender. Sprinkle with the cheese, if using.

Makes 6 servings

Per serving: *287 calories, 33 g protein, 17 g carbohydrates, 9 g fat, 75 mg cholesterol, 460 mg sodium, 2 g dietary fiber*

Diet Exchanges: *0 milk, 1 vegetable, 0 fruit, 1 bread, 4 meat, 1 fat*

SECRETS OF WEIGHT-LOSS WINNERS

• Simple changes like low-cal salad dressing instead of regular and not having fresh bakery bread and butter with every meal made a big difference for my husband and me.

—Ann Painter, Pittsburgh, Pennsylvania

• When eating at McDonald's or Burger King, take baked chips or pretzels with you. You'll have something crunchy and won't feel like you need fries.

—Judy Lanyon, Bald Knob, Arkansas

• For us, the perfect healthy snack is black beans, salsa, and fat-free honey-wheat tortillas.

—Bill and Hillary Bennett, Boca Raton, Florida

Cajun Shrimp Soup

—Valerie Veilleux, Orleans, Ontario

"I use the packaged rings of shrimp when they're on sale and just remove the tails."

1 bulb garlic

1 tablespoon olive oil

4–5 ribs celery, chopped

1 red bell pepper, chopped

1 green bell pepper, chopped

1 small leek, washed and thinly sliced

1 can (28 ounces) diced tomatoes

3 cups water

3 tablespoons chicken bouillon

1 tablespoon Cajun seasoning mix

1 pound medium shrimp, peeled and deveined

Preheat the oven to 350°F.

Place the garlic bulb on a piece of foil, moisten with water, and wrap to seal. Bake for 45 minutes. When cool enough to handle, squeeze the garlic from the bulb.

Heat the oil in a large pot over medium-high heat. Add the garlic, celery, bell peppers, and leek and cook for 10 minutes, or until soft.

Add the tomatoes (with juice), water, bouillon, and seasoning mix and bring just to a boil. Add the shrimp and cook for 5 minutes, or until the shrimp are opaque.

Makes 6 servings

Per serving: *160 calories, 19 g protein, 14 g carbohydrates, 4 g fat, 150 mg cholesterol, 1,000 mg sodium, 4 g dietary fiber*

Diet Exchanges: *0 milk, 2½ vegetable, 0 fruit, 0 bread, 2 meat, ½ fat*

Southwest Chowder

173 Calories

4 ears corn, husks and silks removed

2 dried chipotle chile peppers (wear plastic gloves when handling)

2 teaspoons olive oil

3 ribs celery, chopped

1 onion, chopped

2 cloves garlic, minced

1½ teaspoons ground cumin

5 cups fat-free chicken broth

8 ounces Yukon gold potatoes, cubed

2 bay leaves

1 butternut squash, peeled and cubed

1 roasted red pepper, chopped

¼ cup unbleached all-purpose flour

2 cups 1% milk

8 oyster crackers (optional)

Cook the corn in a large pot of boiling water for 3 minutes, or until tender. Drain and set aside until cool enough to handle. Slice 2 cups kernels off the cobs; reserve the cobs.

Place the chile peppers in a small bowl. Cover with hot water and let stand for 10 minutes, or until soft. Remove and discard the stems and seeds. Mince the peppers; reserve the soaking liquid.

Warm the oil in a large saucepan over medium heat. Add the celery, onion, garlic, and cumin and cook, stirring frequently, for 6 minutes, or until the vegetables are soft and tender. Stir in the broth, potatoes, bay leaves, reserved corn cobs, chipotle soaking liquid, and minced chipotle peppers. Cook for 10 minutes. Add the squash and corn. Cook, stirring occasionally, for 15 minutes, or until the vegetables are tender. Remove and discard the bay leaves and the corn cobs. Stir in the roasted pepper.

Place the flour in a medium bowl. Slowly whisk in the milk until smooth. Stir into the soup and cook, stirring frequently, for 7 minutes, or until slightly thickened. Serve with the oyster crackers, if using.

Makes 8 servings

Per serving: *173 calories, 10 g protein, 30 g carbohydrates, 3 g fat, 5 mg cholesterol, 160 mg sodium, 4 g dietary fiber*

Diet Exchanges: *1/2 milk, 1½ vegetable, 0 fruit, 1 bread, ½ meat, ½ fat*

Carol's Meatless Soup

—Carol Phalin, Arkdale, Wisconsin

"This soup will last throughout the week, and it has very little fat."

1 tablespoon extra-virgin olive oil

1 small onion, chopped

1 rib celery, chopped (including tops)

1 clove garlic, minced

2 cans (8 ounces each) diced tomatoes, drained

6 carrots, chopped

1 small potato, chopped

4 cups water

3 bay leaves

1½ teaspoons dried basil

¾ teaspoon dried oregano

¼ teaspoon salt

¼ teaspoon black pepper

1 cup (6 ounces) elbow macaroni

3 cups shredded cabbage

Heat the oil in a large pot over medium heat. Add the onion, celery, and garlic and cook for 4 minutes, or until tender. Add the tomatoes, carrots, potato, water, bay leaves, basil, oregano, salt, and pepper and bring to a boil. Reduce the heat to low, cover, and simmer for 30 minutes. Add the macaroni and cabbage and cook for 10 minutes, or until the macaroni is al dente and the cabbage is wilted. Remove and discard the bay leaves before serving.

Makes 10 servings

Per serving: *89 calories, 3 g protein, 16 g carbohydrates, 2 g fat, 0 mg cholesterol, 180 mg sodium, 3 g dietary fiber*

Diet Exchanges: *0 milk, 1½ vegetable, 0 fruit, 1 bread, 0 meat, ½ fat*

It Worked for Me!

Jennifer Hoffmann

VITAL STATS

Weight lost: 36 pounds

Time to goal: 5 months

Unique secret to success: Learning to think thin by remembering all the hard work it took to lose weight and making food choices that support and maintain a thinner lifestyle

Losing baby weight seemed impossible for Jennifer. Learning to control portions and increasing her activity once her son was born helped her lose the pregnancy weight—plus even more pounds.

"I quit smoking in anticipation of becoming pregnant—and wound up gaining about 30 pounds. Once I was pregnant, of course, I wasn't supposed to even think of losing weight, and so I didn't.

"After Ryan was born, I tried hard to get back into my old clothes. I starved myself, literally eating nothing the whole day until dinner with my husband. But despite the fact that I was eating so little food, I didn't lose a single pound.

"When my son was about 8 months old, I saw an ad in the newspaper for a local Weight Watchers group that mentioned child-friendly meetings. This made a big difference for me—I would not have been able to go unless I could take Ryan along.

"I followed the guidelines and wound up eating much more food than I had been

eating on my starvation diet, but I still lost 6 pounds the first week. I credit this to portion control. I was able to pretty much eat whatever I wanted to, but in smaller portions. I also learned to make better choices, basically shifting to a low-fat, high-fiber diet.

"I also learned to balance what I ate over time. For example, if I really wanted to have a hamburger for lunch, I would let myself have a small one. But then for dinner, I'd cut back and eat just a salad and maybe a cup of soup. The next day, too, I would be aware of eating a little less. I started to look at my diet overall, not just agonizing over each meal.

"As for exercise, my son is a big boy and very active, so chasing him around keeps me moving. He also loves to be outdoors, so I bought a jogging stroller that I use for long, 2-hour walks two or three times every week.

"Losing almost 40 pounds has made it so much easier to get around with my son. And other new moms want to know how I can be so thin after giving birth. They may not realize all the hard work it took, but the compliments still feel really good to me."

Black Bean Soup

1 tablespoon olive oil

3 carrots, chopped

2 ribs celery, chopped

1 large onion, chopped

3 cloves garlic, minced

2 slices Canadian bacon, cut into bite-size pieces

1 jalapeño chile pepper, seeded and chopped (wear plastic gloves when handling)

1 tablespoon ground cumin

1 can (48 ounces) fat-free chicken broth

1 cup water

2 cans (14–19 ounces each) black beans, rinsed and drained

½ teaspoon salt

Warm the oil in a Dutch oven over medium heat. Add the carrots, celery, onion, and garlic and cook, stirring occasionally, for 4 minutes, or until the onion starts to soften. Add the bacon, chile pepper, and cumin and cook for 3 minutes, or until the bacon is lightly browned. Remove from the pot and set aside.

Add the broth and water. Increase the heat to high and bring to a boil. Reduce the heat to medium-low and cook for 15 minutes, or until the vegetables are tender. Add the beans and cook for 5 minutes, or until heated through.

Ladle 3 cups of the soup into a food processor or blender. Puree until smooth. Return to the pot. Add the reserved bacon mixture and salt. Cook for 5 minutes, or until heated through.

Makes 8 servings

Per serving: *166 calories, 13 g protein, 19 g carbohydrates, 3 g fat, 5 mg cholesterol, 750 mg sodium, 7 g dietary fiber*

Diet Exchanges: *0 milk, 1 vegetable, 0 fruit, 1 bread, 1½ meat, ½ fat*

Kitchen Tip

If desired, stir ¼ cup sherry into the soup along with the beans. The soup can be garnished with chopped onion, chopped fresh cilantro leaves, or a dollop of fat-free sour cream.

Three-Bean Soup

—**Rita Kidd, Martinez, Georgia**

"This recipe freezes really well. I'm on Weight Watchers, and this soup has only one point per cup!"

3 cans (14½ ounces each) diced tomatoes, any style

2 cans (14–19 ounces each) pinto beans, rinsed and drained

1 can (14–19 ounces) New Orleans–style kidney beans, rinsed and drained

1 can (12 ounces) green beans, drained

1 can (11 ounces) fiesta-style corn

1 packet (1¼ ounces) taco seasoning mix

1 packet (1 ounce) dry ranch salad dressing mix

In a large pot over medium-high heat, combine the tomatoes (with juice), pinto beans, kidney beans, green beans, corn, taco seasoning mix, and dressing mix and bring to a boil. Reduce the heat to low, cover, and simmer for 1 hour.

Makes 10 servings

Per serving: *145 calories, 7 g protein, 30 g carbohydrates, 1 g fat, 0 mg cholesterol, 910 mg sodium, 9 g dietary fiber*

Diet Exchanges: *0 milk, 1½ vegetable, 0 fruit, 1½ bread, 0 meat, 0 fat*

Broccoli, Bean, and Pasta Soup

—**Debra Gluck, Mississauga, Ontario**

"Quick and easy, this soup can also be made with cauliflower or white kidney beans, or whatever is on hand. It's very filling and healthy."

10 cups water

16 ounces bow-tie or medium shell pasta

2 packets or cubes (2 teaspoons) chicken bouillon

1 bunch broccoli, cut into florets

2 tablespoons olive oil

1 bunch scallions, chopped

1 can (14–19 ounces) kidney beans

2 tablespoons grated Parmesan cheese

Bring the water to a boil in a large pot. Add the pasta and bouillon and cook for 15 minutes, adding the broccoli during the last 5 minutes of cooking time. Do not drain.

Heat the oil in a medium skillet over medium-high heat. Add the scallions and cook for 2 minutes. Add the beans (with liquid). Reduce the heat to low, cover, and simmer for 5 minutes. Add to the pasta mixture and sprinkle with the cheese.

Makes 8 servings

Per serving: *299 calories, 11 g protein, 52 g carbohydrates, 5 g fat, 0 mg cholesterol, 570 mg sodium, 2 g dietary fiber*

Diet Exchanges: *0 milk, 0 vegetable, 0 fruit, 2½ bread, 0 meat, 1 fat*

Easy Minestrone

—Dawn Biebl, Sidney, Montana

"I am a soup lover. This soup makes me feel full so I'm not likely to snack a couple hours after I eat. I feel good knowing that I am getting veggies and beans—two things that are really good for a healthy diet. Also, my family loves this soup, and I know they are getting a healthful meal."

1 tablespoon olive oil

3 ribs celery, chopped

1 onion, chopped

3 cups water

3 packets or cubes (3 teaspoons) beef bouillon

1 can (28 ounces) whole tomatoes, chopped

2 teaspoons dried basil

2 teaspoons chopped parsley

1 teaspoon dried oregano

½ teaspoon black pepper

1 bay leaf

2 medium potatoes, chopped

2 medium carrots, chopped

2 cans (14–19 ounces each) kidney beans, rinsed and drained

½ cup small shell pasta

Parmesan cheese and/or sour cream

Heat the oil in a medium saucepan over medium heat. Add the celery and onion and cook for 10 minutes, or until soft but not brown. Add the water, bouillon, tomatoes (with juice), basil, parsley, oregano, pepper, and bay leaf. Bring to a boil. Reduce the heat to low, cover, and simmer for 25 minutes.

Add the potatoes and carrots, cover, and simmer for 15 minutes, or until the vegetables are tender. Add the beans and pasta and cook for 12 minutes, or until the pasta is al dente. Remove and discard the bay leaf. Serve with a sprinkling of cheese or a swirl of sour cream.

Makes 12 servings

Per serving: *120 calories, 6 g protein, 23 g carbohydrates, 2 g fat, 0 mg cholesterol, 440 mg sodium, 5 g dietary fiber*

Diet Exchanges: *0 milk, 1 vegetable, 0 fruit, 1 bread, 0 meat, 0 fat*

Carrot Soup

—Jennifer Jensen, Riceville, Iowa

"Don't let the everyday staples in this recipe fool you into thinking it will be bland. This is a rich soup that even my children—ages 2, 5, 7, and 9—gobble up. I eat this with a turkey sandwich on whole wheat bread and a small salad for a healthy and filling lunch. Eating healthy doesn't have to be boring!"

    4 cups vegetable broth
 1½ teaspoons salt
    1 pound carrots, chopped
    1 large potato, peeled and chopped
    1 large onion, chopped
    1 teaspoon dried basil, crumbled
   ⅛ teaspoon black pepper
    1 tablespoon butter or margarine, softened

Place the broth and salt in a 3-quart saucepan and bring to a boil over high heat. Add the carrots, potato, and onion. Reduce the heat to low, cover, and simmer for 10 minutes, or until the vegetables are tender. Place the vegetables and cooking water in a blender or food processor and process until pureed.

Return the puree to the saucepan. Add the basil and pepper and heat through. Stir in the butter or margarine just before serving.

Makes 4 servings

Per serving: *110 calories, 3 g protein, 19 g carbohydrates, 4 g fat, 8 mg cholesterol, 780 mg sodium, 3 g dietary fiber*

Diet Exchanges: *0 milk, 2½ vegetable, 0 fruit, 0 bread, 0 meat, 1 fat*

Kitchen Tip

To speed up the prep time, you can chop the vegetables separately in a food processor rather than slicing them by hand.

Italian Mushroom Soup

—Ann Painter, Pittsburgh

"We eat a small bowl of this soup every day with dinner as a filler."

2 tablespoons olive oil

1 bulb garlic, chopped

1 large onion, chopped

2 pounds sliced mushrooms or 4 cans (8 ounces each) sliced mushrooms, drained

3 cans (14½ ounces each) diced tomatoes

4 cups water

4 packets or cubes (4 teaspoons) chicken bouillon

2 tablespoons chopped parsley

2 teaspoons dried Italian seasoning

¼ teaspoon coarsely ground black pepper

2 drops hot-pepper sauce

Dash of Worcestershire sauce

Heat the oil in a large pot over medium-high heat. Add the garlic and onion and cook, stirring, for 3 minutes, or until soft. Add the mushrooms and tomatoes (with juice), water, bouillon, parsley, Italian seasoning, black pepper, hot-pepper sauce, and Worcestershire sauce and cook for 30 minutes, or until the mushrooms are tender.

Makes 6 servings

Per serving: *77 calories, 3 g protein, 10 g carbohydrates, 3 g fat, 0 mg cholesterol, 891 mg sodium, 2 g dietary fiber*

Diet Exchanges: *0 milk, 2 vegetable, 0 fruit, 0 bread, 0 meat, 0 fat*

Four-Vinegar Salad Dressing

—Virginia Kerbs, Woodacre, California

"My children tell me I should bottle this dressing. Everyone I serve it to loves it. Serve over cut romaine with crumbled feta or blue cheese, sliced almonds or pecans, and dried cranberries."

⅓ **cup seasoned rice wine vinegar**

⅓ **cup raspberry vinegar**

2 **tablespoons red wine vinegar**

2 **tablespoons balsamic vinegar**

¼ **cup extra-virgin olive oil or to taste**

1 **clove garlic, minced**

½ **teaspoon Dijon mustard**

½ **teaspoon sugar**

½ **teaspoon salt**

½ **teaspoon black pepper**

In a jar with a tight-fitting lid, combine the vinegars, oil, garlic, mustard, sugar, salt, and pepper. Seal the jar and shake well.

Makes 24 servings (1 tablespoon each)

Per tablespoon: *26 calories, 0 protein, 1 g carbohydrates, 2 g fat, 0 mg cholesterol, 118 mg sodium, 0 g dietary fiber*

Diet Exchanges: *0 milk, 0 vegetable, 0 fruit, 0 bread, 0 meat, ½ fat*

CURB CRAVINGS WITH OIL

Adding a Mediterranean staple—flavorful full-fat olive oil—to your diet may help you control cravings. In a Pennsylvania State University study led by Steve E. Specter, Ph.D., men who ate a lunch that included mashed potatoes prepared with monounsaturated oil such as olive oil stayed satisfied longer than when the potatoes contained polyunsaturated oil such as corn oil.

And Marshall Goldberg, M.D., an endocrinologist at Thomas Jefferson University Medical College in Philadelphia, found that a concentrated dose of olive oil—2 teaspoons on half a slice of bread, eaten 15 to 20 minutes before a meal—helps his patients control their cravings too.

Researchers think olive oil may slow stomach contractions, which creates a sense of fullness, and it stimulates the release of cholecystokinin (CCK), a gut hormone that signals the brain to stop eating. Some people have reported that an olive oil appetizer quieted prelunch stomach growlings or filled them up so they ate less at lunch.

Just remember that olive oil contains 40 calories per teaspoon, so stick to small amounts and one small slice of bread for dipping.

Fruit 'n' Spinach Salad

—Crystal Burlow, Greensboro, North Carolina

"My husband doesn't even like spinach, but loves this as a meal. I serve it with a slice of bread or roll, and it hits the spot. Low in calories but high in nutrition and taste, it has helped us both lose weight."

SALAD

- 6 cups (8 ounces) fresh spinach, torn
- ½ cantaloupe, cut into bite-size pieces
- 1 cup strawberries, hulled and sliced
- 1 cup fresh pineapple chunks

DRESSING

- 2 tablespoons seedless raspberry jam
- 2 tablespoons raspberry white wine vinegar
- 1 tablespoon honey
- 2 teaspoons olive oil
- ¼ cup halved or chopped walnuts

To make the salad:

In a large serving bowl, combine the spinach, cantaloupe, strawberries, and pineapple.

To make the dressing:

In a small bowl, whisk together the jam, vinegar, honey, and oil. Drizzle over the spinach mixture and toss to coat. Sprinkle with the walnuts.

Makes 6 servings

Per serving: *123 calories, 2 g protein, 19 g carbohydrates, 5 g fat, 0 mg cholesterol, 30 mg sodium, 3 g dietary fiber*

Diet Exchanges: *0 milk, 0 vegetable, ½ fruit, ½ bread, 0 meat, 1 fat*

Fresh and Filling Luncheon Salad

160 Calories

—Patricia Nairne, Winnipeg, Manitoba

"I don't feel deprived with this salad as there is a lot of texture and flavor. The rice cakes give me the crunch that I used to get from croutons. I have also used garbanzo beans or kidney beans instead of the protein."

¼ cup low-fat mayonnaise salad dressing

2 tablespoons lemon juice or balsamic vinegar

¼ teaspoon black pepper

1 head romaine lettuce, torn

1 cup sliced cooked chicken or beef

1 carrot, thinly sliced

1 tomato, coarsely chopped

½ small cucumber, sliced

2 tablespoons Parmesan cheese (optional)

1 tablespoon crumbled blue cheese

1 tablespoon sunflower seeds (optional)

2 brown rice cakes, crumbled

In a measuring cup, combine the salad dressing, lemon juice or vinegar, and pepper.

In a large serving bowl, combine the lettuce, chicken or beef, carrot, tomato, cucumber, Parmesan (if using), blue cheese, and sunflower seeds (if using). Sprinkle with the rice cakes and drizzle with the dressing. Toss to coat evenly.

Makes 4 servings

Per serving: *160 calories, 12 g protein, 13 g carbohydrates, 8 g fat, 30 mg cholesterol, 220 mg sodium, 3 g dietary fiber*

Diet Exchanges: *0 milk, 1½ vegetable, 0 fruit, 0 bread, 1½ meat, ½ fat*

Fabulous 5-Minute Coleslaw

150 Calories

—Gail Hayes, Breckenridge, Minnesota

"This works as a great midmeal snack for me—lots of fiber to fill me up and enough sweet to satisfy my craving."

2 cups preshredded cabbage or coleslaw mixture
2 cups broccoli slaw mixture, chopped slightly
¼ cup golden raisins
¼ cup almonds, slivered
½–⅔ cup fat-free poppyseed salad dressing

In a large serving bowl, combine the cabbage mixture, broccoli slaw, raisins, almonds, and salad dressing. Toss to coat evenly.

Makes 4 servings

Per serving: *150 calories, 4 g protein, 24 g carbohydrates, 5 g fat, 0 mg cholesterol, 380 mg sodium, 4 g dietary fiber*

Diet Exchanges: *0 milk, 1 vegetable, 0 fruit, 1 bread, ½ meat, 1 fat*

SHOPPING SAVVY

Crunch a Bunch

Here's a snack that's an excellent sub for fatty chips. Pita-Snax—made from pita dough—are low in calories and fat, and they're cholesterol-free. Compared with a 1-ounce serving of ordinary chips, you can have 34 Pita-Snax versus about 13 chips, you'll take in 110 calories rather than 150, and you'll get just 1½ grams of fat instead of about 10. Try Lightly Salted, Garlic, Dill Ranch, Cheddar Cheese, Chili and Lime, and Cinnamon. Look for Pita-Snax in major supermarkets or online at www.pitasnax.com.

Red Cabbage with Apples

—Rose Nicolini, Lighthouse Point, Florida

"You'll feel like you're cheating with this recipe, because of the delicious apples and cinnamon!"

1 tablespoon extra-virgin olive oil

1 Granny Smith apple, halved, cored, and cubed

1 bag (10 ounces) shredded red cabbage

½ cup water

4 tablespoons sugar-free maple syrup

2 tablespoons white balsamic vinegar

½ teaspoon ground cinnamon

Heat the oil in a large skillet over medium-high heat. Add the apple and cook, stirring occasionally, for 5 minutes. Add the cabbage, water, maple syrup, vinegar, and cinnamon. Reduce the heat to low and cook, stirring occasionally, for 20 minutes, or until the cabbage is tender-crisp.

Makes 4 servings

Per serving: *78 calories, 1 g protein, 13 g carbohydrates, 4 g fat, 0 mg cholesterol, 35 mg sodium, 2 g dietary fiber*

Diet Exchanges: *0 milk, 1 vegetable, ½ fruit, ½ bread, 0 meat, 0 fat*

Apple and Cabbage Salad

—Patsy Roy, Belledune, New Brunswick

"I lost 14 pounds last year from May to September from walking, eating right, and having this salad every day with one of my meals."

6 tablespoons cider vinegar

2 tablespoons olive oil

1 teaspoon mustard

½ teaspoon honey or sugar

Pinch of black pepper

6 cups shredded red cabbage

2 apples with skin, cored and diced

In a large bowl, combine the vinegar, oil, mustard, honey or sugar, and pepper. Add the cabbage and apples and toss to coat well. Refrigerate before serving.

Makes 16 servings

Per serving: *34 calories, 1 g protein, 5 g carbohydrates, 2 g fat, 0 mg cholesterol, 5 mg sodium, 1 g dietary fiber*

Diet Exchanges: *0 milk, ½ vegetable, 0 fruit, 0 bread, 0 meat, 0 fat*

Cooked Zucchini Salad

—Yona Shapiro, New Hempstead, New York

*" I use this salad to help me get my nine fruits and vegetables a day.
As a mother of six children, losing weight isn't an easy job, but I'm working on it! "*

1 teaspoon canola oil
1 medium onion, chopped
3 medium tomatoes, chopped
3 medium zucchini, quartered and sliced
½ teaspoon Italian seasoning
¼ teaspoon salt

Heat the oil in a medium skillet over medium-high heat. Add the onion and cook, stirring, for 3 minutes, or until soft. Add the tomatoes and zucchini and cook, stirring, for 5 minutes, or until tender. Sprinkle with the Italian seasoning and salt. Reduce the heat to medium-low and cook, stirring occasionally, for 1 hour.

Makes 4 servings

Per serving: *64 calories, 3 g protein, 12 g carbohydrates, 2 g fat, 0 mg cholesterol, 199 mg sodium, 4 g dietary fiber*

Diet Exchanges: *0 milk, 1½ vegetable, 0 fruit, ½ bread, 0 meat, ½ fat*

SHOPPING SAVVY

Make the Most of Salads

Turned off by lackluster salads served at fast-food outlets? Turn to delicious organic Laptop Salads from Melissa's/ World Variety Produce. With flavors like Asian Soy, Grilled Veggie, Caesar, and Spinach, you'll never steer into another drive-thru! Salads come complete with dressing, vegetables, and toppers, and ingredients run the gamut from organic greens, white rice, and tofu to edamame, tomatoes, croutons, and Parmesan cheese. Visit www.melissas.com to find a store near you that carries these fantastic, filling salads.

Hoppin' John Salad

299 Calories

2 slices turkey bacon

1 onion, chopped

2 cloves garlic, minced

3 cups fat-free chicken broth

½ cup wild rice, rinsed

1 teaspoon dried thyme

½ cup long-grain white rice

1 cup frozen black-eyed peas, thawed

1 rib celery, chopped

½ green bell pepper, chopped

1 small tomato, chopped

¼ cup chopped Italian parsley

2 tablespoons lemon juice

½ teaspoon hot-pepper sauce

¼ teaspoon black pepper

⅛ teaspoon salt

4 large beefsteak tomatoes

Cook the bacon in a medium saucepan over medium-high heat for 2 minutes, or until crisp. Remove from the pan and set aside until cool; crumble.

Add the onion and garlic to the same pan. Cook for 4 minutes, or until softened. Add the broth, wild rice, and thyme and bring to a boil. Cover, reduce the heat to low, and cook for 20 minutes.

Add the white rice. Cover and cook for 20 minutes, or until the rice is tender. Fluff the rice with a fork, loosely cover, and let cool completely.

Stir in the black-eyed peas, celery, bell pepper, chopped tomato, parsley, lemon juice, hot-pepper sauce, black pepper, salt, and crumbled bacon.

Slice the tops from the beefsteak tomatoes; carefully scoop out the insides and discard or reserve for another use. Divide the rice mixture among the tomatoes.

Makes 4 servings

Per serving: *299 calories, 16 g protein, 55 g carbohydrates, 2 g fat, 5 mg cholesterol, 360 mg sodium, 6 g dietary fiber*

Diet Exchanges: *0 milk, 2 vegetable, 0 fruit, 3 bread, 1 meat, 0 fat*

Kitchen Tip

You can replace the frozen black-eyed peas with 1 cup rinsed and drained canned black-eyed peas.

Favorite Bean Salad

—Karen Paulsen, Davis, California

"This is super-fast to prepare and tastes great! I never get sick of it because it's always changing, depending on what's available and what combination of ingredients sounds good. This salad is whatever I want it to be, depending on my mood! It's also low in fat, high in nutrition, and very satisfying."

½ cup balsamic vinegar

¼ cup orange juice or other fruit juice

1 teaspoon extra-virgin olive oil

1 tablespoon mustard or prepared pesto

1 tablespoon chopped fresh herbs, such as chives and parsley

¼ teaspoon salt

⅛ teaspoon black pepper

2 cans (14–19 ounces) beans, such as black, cannellini, and/or kidney, rinsed and drained

1 cup corn kernels

1 tomato, chopped

1 green or yellow bell pepper, chopped

½ red onion, chopped

Per serving: *140 calories, 7 g protein, 27 g carbohydrates, 1 g fat, 0 mg cholesterol, 180 mg sodium, 2 g dietary fiber*

Diet Exchanges: *0 milk, 1 vegetable, 0 fruit, ½ bread, 0 meat, 0 fat*

In a large serving bowl, combine the vinegar, orange juice, oil, mustard or pesto, herbs, salt, and black pepper. Add the beans, corn, tomato, bell pepper, and onion and toss to coat.

Makes 8 servings

Corn and Bean Salad

—Natasha Marchewka, Folsom, California

"This recipe has protein, carbs, and vegetables, so it's a balanced meal that helps keep my hunger pangs at bay. It's easy to grab as a meal or a snack."

½ cup wild rice

1 can (11 ounces) low-sodium whole kernel corn, drained

1 can (14–19 ounces) black beans, rinsed and drained

2 green onions, chopped

½ small red bell pepper, chopped

1 small bunch fresh cilantro, chopped

Juice of 1 lemon

¼ teaspoon salt

⅛ teaspoon black pepper

Prepare the rice according to package directions.

Meanwhile, in a serving bowl, combine the corn, beans, onions, bell pepper, cilantro, lemon juice, salt, and pepper. Add the rice and toss to combine.

Makes 6 servings

Per serving: *125 calories, 6 g protein, 29 g carbohydrates, 1 g fat, 0 mg cholesterol, 315 mg sodium, 5 g dietary fiber*

Diet Exchanges: *0 milk, ½ vegetable, 0 fruit, 1½ bread, 0 meat, 0 fat*

SECRETS OF WEIGHT-LOSS WINNERS

• Eating oatmeal every morning helped my husband lose 55 pounds—*and* drop his cholesterol by 60 points.

—**Donna Greer, Lenoir, North Carolina**

• For snacking, I have just a few small pretzels and drink water with a squirt of lemon juice. This is especially good when I'm watching a movie.

—**Judy Lanyon, Bald Knob, Arkansas**

• Simple switches like replacing refined carbs with whole grain ones, eating smaller meals several times a day, and using low-sodium recipes have given me the beginning of a healthier and thinner lifestyle.

—**Bobbie Miller, Washington, Pennsylvania**

Lentil Salad

245 Calories

¾ cup green or brown lentils, rinsed and drained

1 shallot, halved lengthwise

¼ teaspoon ground cloves

2 plum tomatoes, chopped

2 ribs celery, chopped

½ yellow bell pepper, chopped

½ red onion, finely chopped

3 ounces goat cheese, crumbled

2 tablespoons chopped parsley

2 tablespoons chopped fresh mint

3 tablespoons lemon juice

1 teaspoon honey

1 teaspoon olive oil

1 clove garlic, minced

Salt and black pepper

Place the lentils in a medium saucepan and cover with 3" of water. Add the shallot and cloves and bring to a boil over high heat. Reduce the heat to low, cover, and simmer for 20 minutes, or until the lentils are tender. Drain in a colander and discard the shallots. Set the lentils aside to cool.

In a large bowl, combine the tomatoes, celery, bell pepper, onion, cheese, parsley, and mint. Stir in the lentils.

In a small bowl, combine the lemon juice, honey, oil, and garlic. Pour over the salad and gently toss to combine. Season with the salt and black pepper.

Makes 4 servings

Per serving: *245 calories, 16 g protein, 30 g carbohydrates, 8 g fat, 15 mg cholesterol, 135 mg sodium, 13 g dietary fiber*

Diet Exchanges: *0 milk, 1 vegetable, 0 fruit, 2 bread, 1 meat, 1 fat*

Italian Pasta Salad

—Christy Kishel, Valencia, California

1 box (16 ounces) rainbow rotini
2 medium carrots, chopped
2 stalks broccoli, cut into florets
1 bottle (8 ounces) low-fat Italian dressing

Prepare the pasta according to package directions. Rinse and drain. Place in a serving bowl and refrigerate for 20 minutes.

Add the carrots and broccoli to the bowl and toss to combine. Add the dressing and toss to coat.

Makes 8 servings

Per serving: *252 calories, 8 g protein, 47 g carbohydrates, 4 g fat, 0 mg cholesterol, 240 mg sodium, 3 g dietary fiber*

Diet Exchanges: *0 milk, 1 vegetable, 0 fruit, 3 bread, 0 meat, 1/2 fat*

Kitchen Tip

This is a versatile recipe that can take on different flavors in a snap. Try low-fat ranch dressing with red bell pepper strips and snow peas, or Thousand Island dressing with cauliflower and sweet peas.

Ceviche Salad

—Bobby Ruiz, Woodstock, Georgia

"I eat this delicious dish once a week."

3 tomatoes, seeded and chopped

1 cucumber, peeled, halved, seeded, and chopped

1 red onion, chopped

¼ cup chopped fresh cilantro

½ pound peeled, deveined, and cooked shrimp, chopped

½ pound lump crabmeat, drained

¼ cup freshly squeezed lime juice

In a large serving bowl, combine the tomatoes, cucumber, onion, cilantro, shrimp, and crabmeat. Sprinkle with the lime juice and gently stir to combine. Refrigerate for at least 30 minutes.

Makes 6 servings

Per serving: *100 calories, 16 g protein, 7 g carbohydrates, 1 g fat, 105 mg cholesterol, 210 mg sodium, 2 g dietary fiber*

Diet Exchanges: *0 milk, 1½ vegetable, 0 fruit, 0 bread, 1 meat, 0 fat*

Kitchen Tip

This dish is perfect served with low-fat baked corn chips.

Tuna-Pasta Salad

213 Calories

4 ounces rigatoni

¼ cup fat-free chicken broth

2 tablespoons lemon juice

1 tablespoon chopped fresh oregano

2 teaspoons extra-virgin olive oil

2 cloves garlic, minced

½ teaspoon sugar

¼ teaspoon black pepper

1 can (4 ounces) water-packed solid white tuna, drained and flaked

4 ounces frozen artichoke hearts, thawed and patted dry

3 scallions, thinly sliced

1 roasted red pepper, chopped

¼ cup (1 ounce) crumbled feta cheese

Prepare the pasta according to package directions. Drain and place in a large bowl. Let cool for 10 minutes.

In a small bowl, whisk together the broth, lemon juice, oregano, oil, garlic, sugar, and black pepper. Pour over the pasta. Add the tuna, artichokes, scallions, roasted pepper, and cheese. Toss to combine.

Makes 4 servings

Per serving: *213 calories, 13 g protein, 29 g carbohydrates, 5 g fat, 20 mg cholesterol, 125 mg sodium, 4 g dietary fiber*

Diet Exchanges: *0 milk, 1 vegetable, 0 fruit, 1½ bread, 1½ meat, 1 fat*

Kitchen Tip

To create your own spinoffs of this recipe, try substituting cooked chicken, turkey breast, crabmeat, or shrimp for the tuna. Add steamed green beans or wax beans, diced tomatoes, chopped cooked egg whites, rinsed capers, or your favorite fresh herbs.

WHICH LOW-FAT FOODS TASTE BEST?

If eating low-fat foods makes you feel like you're making a sacrifice, you may not be choosing the right foods. When S. E. Specter, Ph.D., and fellow researchers at Pennsylvania State University in State College had 26 men eat a variety of reduced-fat foods (75 percent less fat than the standard versions), they discovered that certain types of low-fat foods were more appetizing.

Foods that gain appeal even when you cut the fat include creamy foods such as tuna salad and chocolate pudding and oily foods such as potato chips.

Foods that may lose appeal when you cut the fat include ground beef and yellow cake. For these types of foods, you might want to try having the full-fat version now and then—just keep your portions under control.

Pan-Seared Scallop Salad

293 Calories

VINAIGRETTE

¾ cup lime juice

¼ cup balsamic vinegar

1 tablespoon honey

1 tablespoon olive oil

Salt and black pepper

SALAD

1½ cups thawed and chopped frozen artichoke hearts

2 plum tomatoes, chopped

1 medium seedless cucumber, chopped

1 tablespoon minced shallots

5 cups mesclun or spring mix salad

1 pound jumbo sea scallops

1 teaspoon black pepper

To make the vinaigrette:

In a small bowl, whisk together the lime juice, vinegar, honey, and oil. Season to taste with salt and pepper.

To make the salad:

In a medium bowl, combine the artichokes, tomatoes, cucumber, and shallots. Add half of the vinaigrette and toss to coat.

Place the mesclun or salad mix in a large bowl. Add the remaining vinaigrette and toss to coat.

Place a large nonstick skillet coated with cooking spray over medium-high heat. Sprinkle the scallops with the pepper. Add to the skillet and cook for 2 minutes per side, or until opaque.

Divide the lettuce mixture among 4 plates. Top with the artichoke mixture and the scallops.

Makes 4 servings

Per serving: *293 calories, 34 g protein, 26 g carbohydrates, 5 g fat, 75 mg cholesterol, 400 mg sodium, 7 g dietary fiber*

Diet Exchanges: *0 milk, 2½ vegetable, ½ fruit, ½ bread, 4 meat, 1 fat*

Kitchen Tip

The vinaigrette can also double as a marinade for chicken or firm-fleshed fish, such as swordfish, halibut, or tuna.

Avocado Chicken Salad

—Shelby Chassell, Nacogdoches, Texas

2 avocados, mashed

2 tablespoons fat-free plain yogurt

1 tablespoon lime juice or lemon juice

½ teaspoon garlic salt

¼ teaspoon hot-pepper sauce (optional)

1 cup thinly sliced cooked chicken breast

1 tomato, chopped

4 whole wheat tortillas (8" in diameter)

Mash the avocados in a medium bowl. Add the yogurt, lime juice or lemon juice, garlic salt, and hot-pepper sauce (if using), and stir to combine. Add the chicken and tomato and toss to blend. Evenly divide the salad among the tortillas. Roll up and serve.

Makes 4 servings

Per serving: *347 calories, 27 g protein, 27 g carbohydrates, 18 g fat, 60 mg cholesterol, 360 mg sodium, 2 g dietary fiber*

Diet Exchanges: *0 milk, ½ vegetable, 0 fruit, 1 bread, 3 meat, ½ fat*

Chicken-Broccoli Salad

—Cathy Belliveau, Clintonville, Wisconsin

"This recipe is fast, easy, and low-fat."

1 package (3½ ounces) chicken-flavored ramen noodles

2 cups cooked and sliced chicken breast

1 package (16 ounces) broccoli slaw

½ cup fat-free mayonnaise

½ cup sliced almonds

Prepare the noodles according to package directions, using half the water called for. Place in a serving bowl. Add the chicken, broccoli slaw, almonds, and mayonnaise and toss to coat. Serve immediately or chill.

Makes 4 servings

Per serving: *282 calories, 25 g protein, 13 g carbohydrates, 15 g fat, 59 mg cholesterol, 218 mg sodium, 5 g dietary fiber*

Diet Exchanges: *0 milk, 0 vegetable, 0 fruit, 1 bread, 2½ meat, 2 fat*

It Worked for Me!

Carole DeMartino

VITAL STATS

Weight lost: 120 pounds

Time to goal: 2 years

Unique secret to success: Replaced a food addiction and repeated attempts at fad dieting with a new approach: healthy choices and moderation

Carole grew up in a "clean your plate" family. Her weight quickly became—and stayed—a problem. When Carole finally realized that fad diets were the road to failure, she started to lose weight the sensible way.

"At work I would starve myself and eat nothing, or else delicately nibble a salad for lunch. But once I got home I would eat with wild abandon: an entire bag of chips with sour cream on the side, a towering stack of crackers with peanut butter and marshmallow, plus a full spaghetti-and-meatball dinner, followed by butter almond ice cream, popcorn, nuts, and more. I was addicted to food.

"To lose weight I would turn to any and every fad diet out there. You name it, I've tried it. Once I fasted for 9 months, existing on nothing but coffee, corn, and rice. Sure, I lost 120 pounds, but I also developed ulcers and gained all the weight back—plus even more. I resigned myself to the 'fact' that I'd be heavy forever.

"My wake-up call came in July 1994, when I stepped on a scale at the hospital where I worked. The needle hit a shocking 265 pounds, and a horrible feeling came over me. As a medical technologist, I knew my weight could kill me—I was already borderline diabetic with a cholesterol level of 270 and was taking hypertension medication.

"The seriousness of the situation gave me a new resolve. I ate nothing but fruits, vegetables, and fish for the next 2 weeks, limiting my choices but eating as much as I wanted so I wouldn't feel hungry. I knew I wanted this change to last, so I soon added whole grains, low-fat dairy, beans, and nuts. Oddly, I found that I had stopped craving meat.

"My plan was simple: Make only healthy choices and use moderation. This was a drastic change from the strict diets I had tried to follow in the past.

"I also tried something I had never done before as an adult: exercise. I walked and walked, seeking out hills for more muscle toning and pacing in the mall when it rained. Eventually, I added 30 minutes of strength training.

"In just 2 years, I lost 120 pounds, lowered my cholesterol without medication, and took 15 inches off my waist. At 58, I can honestly say I look and feel better than I ever have in my life."

Mediterranean Vegetables with Beans

125 Calories

4 medium zucchini and/or yellow squash, sliced diagonally ¼" thick

4 carrots, peeled and sliced diagonally ¼" thick

1 red onion, cut into wedges

1 red bell pepper, seeded and cut into ½"-wide strips

2 tablespoons fat-free chicken broth

1 tablespoon red wine vinegar

1½ teaspoons olive oil

1½ teaspoons Dijon mustard

1 clove garlic, minced

1 teaspoon sugar

1 teaspoon dried basil

¼ teaspoon salt

1 can (14–19 ounces) cannellini beans, rinsed and drained

Coat a grill rack or broiler-pan rack with cooking spray. Preheat the grill or broiler.

Lightly coat the zucchini and/or yellow squash, carrots, onion, and bell pepper with cooking spray. Place on the prepared rack and grill or broil, turning occasionally, for 8 minutes, or until tender.

Meanwhile, in a large bowl, combine the broth, vinegar, oil, mustard, garlic, sugar, basil, and salt. Whisk to blend. Add the beans. Remove the grilled vegetables to the bowl with the beans. Toss to combine.

Makes 6 servings

Per serving: *125 calories, 7 g protein, 26 g carbohydrates, 2 g fat, 0 mg cholesterol, 400 mg sodium, 8 g dietary fiber*

Diet Exchanges: *0 milk, 3 vegetable, 0 fruit, ½ bread, 0 meat, 0 fat*

Brown Rice with Peppers and Zucchini

210 Calories

—Arlene Maney, Whittier, North Carolina

"Brown rice is so filling and the vegetables are so colorful that this dish is very pleasing to the eye and therefore, the stomach. It can be varied by using different veggies and even adding chicken, so that I can make several different-tasting dishes using the same basic recipe."

½ cup quick-cooking brown rice

1 packet or cube (1 teaspoon) beef or chicken bouillon

1 tablespoon olive oil

½ each red and yellow bell pepper, thinly sliced (¾ cup each)

½ zucchini, thinly sliced

1 tablespoon dried cilantro

½ teaspoon dried basil

½ teaspoon salt

Prepare the rice according to package directions, adding the bouillon to the water instead of salt.

Meanwhile, heat the oil in a large skillet over low heat. Add the bell peppers, zucchini, cilantro, basil, and salt. Increase the heat to medium and cook, stirring, for 3 minutes, or until crisp-tender. Serve the vegetables over the rice.

Makes 2 servings

Per serving: *210 calories, 4 g protein, 32 g carbohydrates, 8 g fat, 0 mg cholesterol, 1,020 mg sodium, 4 g dietary fiber*

Diet Exchanges: *0 milk, 1 vegetable, 0 fruit, 2 bread, 0 meat, 0 fat*

Kitchen Tip

Use the remaining pepper halves and zucchini by tossing into tomorrow's dinner salad. Or, serve as a side dish the next day—simply toss with a tablespoon of olive oil in a baking dish, season to taste, and roast for 15 minutes.

FAST TRADES FOR FAST FOODS

According to research from the University of Minnesota, cutting back on your favorite fast foods can help you lose up to 23 pounds a year without doing anything else. Here's how.

Fast-food favorite	Better bet	Have your fave twice a week and the better bet twice, and you can . . .	Have the better bet four times a week, and you can . . .
French fries, large (533 calories)	Potato chips, 1-ounce snack-size bag (150 calories)	Save 766 calories a week; lose 12 pounds in a year	Save 1,532 calories a week; lose 23 pounds in a year
Fried chicken, breast and wing (494 calories)	Roasted chicken breast and thigh without skin (251 calories)	Save 486 calories a week; lose 7 pounds in a year	Save 972 calories a week; lose 15 pounds in a year
Burger (306 calories)	Meat-style veggie burger (90 calories)	Save 432 calories a week; lose 7 pounds in a year	Save 864 calories a week; lose 13 pounds in a year
Bacon (3 slices) and eggs (2, any style) (299 calories)	Deli-style ham (2 slices) and egg substitute (100 calories)	Save 398 calories a week; lose 6 pounds in a year	Save 796 calories a week; lose 12 pounds in a year
Hot dog (180 calories)	Light (95% fat-free) beef hot dog (55 calories)	Save 250 calories a week; lose 4 pounds in a year	Save 500 calories a week; lose 8 pounds in a year

Sweet-Potato Gnocchi with Sage Sauce

360 Calories

8 tablespoons semolina flour

1 pound sweet potatoes, peeled and cut into $\frac{1}{2}$" cubes

$\frac{1}{4}$ cup liquid egg substitute

1 tablespoon chopped fresh thyme

$\frac{1}{4}$ teaspoon salt

$\frac{1}{4}$ teaspoon ground nutmeg

$\frac{1}{2}$ cup + 1 tablespoon unbleached all-purpose flour

$\frac{1}{4}$ cup + 2 tablespoons grated Parmesan cheese

1 cup fat-free chicken broth

3 leaves fresh sage, chopped

$\frac{2}{3}$ cup fat-free nondairy creamer

Black pepper

Evenly dust 2 baking sheets with 2 table-spoons of the semolina flour.

Place the sweet potatoes in a large saucepan. Cover with cold water and bring to a boil over high heat. Reduce the heat to medium and cook for 12 minutes, or until tender. Drain and place in a large bowl. Mash until smooth. Let cool for 10 minutes.

Stir in the egg substitute, thyme, salt, and nutmeg. Add $\frac{1}{2}$ cup of the all-purpose flour, $\frac{1}{4}$ cup of the cheese, and the remaining 6 ta-blespoons semolina flour. Mix well. Shape the dough into a ball and divide into 8 por-tions.

On a lightly floured surface, roll out 1 por-tion of the dough at a time into a 16" rope.

Cut into 1" pieces. Place the pieces on the prepared baking sheets.

Bring the broth and sage to a boil in a large saucepan over high heat. Cook for 3 minutes, or until reduced by one-third. Re-duce the heat to medium.

In a small bowl, whisk together the creamer and the remaining 1 tablespoon all-purpose flour. Whisk into the broth with the remaining 2 tablespoons cheese and cook, stirring constantly, for 2 minutes, or until thickened. Season with the pepper. Keep warm over low heat.

Cook the gnocchi in a large pot of boiling water for 45 seconds, or until they float to the surface. Remove with a slotted spoon and place in the pan with the sauce. Stir into the sauce until well-coated.

Makes 4 servings

Per serving: *360 calories, 19 g protein, 58 g car-bohydrates, 5 g fat, 85 mg cholesterol, 470 mg sodium, 4 g dietary fiber*

Diet Exchanges: *0 milk, 0 vegetable, 0 fruit, $3\frac{1}{2}$ bread, 2 meat, $\frac{1}{2}$ fat*

Kitchen Tip

Look for semolina flour in the baking section of large supermarkets and Italian grocery stores. If you can't find it, all-purpose flour can be substituted.

If desired, top each serving with a light dusting of additional grated Parmesan cheese.

Pasta with Veggie Sauce

—Susan Malbrough, Slidell, Louisiana

"This colorful sauce is very low in fat and high in taste. It fills us up fast!"

 1 zucchini, sliced
 1 yellow squash, sliced
 1 large onion, chopped
 1 large green bell pepper, chopped
 6 cloves garlic, crushed
12 Roma tomatoes, sliced
 1 can (28 ounces) whole tomatoes, chopped
 2 packages Splenda (2 teaspoons)
 2 tablespoons Italian seasoning
 2 teaspoons dried basil
 2 bay leaves
 $\frac{1}{2}$ teaspoon salt
 $\frac{1}{4}$ teaspoon black pepper
12 ounces vegetable or spinach linguine

Heat a large saucepan coated with cooking spray over medium heat. Add the zucchini, yellow squash, onion, bell pepper, and garlic and cook, stirring frequently, for 10 minutes, or until the vegetables are soft. Add the sliced tomatoes, canned tomatoes (with juice), Splenda, Italian seasoning, basil, bay leaves, salt, and pepper and simmer for 30 minutes to blend the flavors. Remove and discard the bay leaves.

Meanwhile, prepare the pasta according to package directions. Serve the vegetable sauce over the pasta.

Makes 6 servings

Per serving: *290 calories, 11 g protein, 61 g carbohydrates, 2 g fat, 0 mg cholesterol, 750 mg sodium, 7 g dietary fiber*

Diet Exchanges: *0 milk, 3 vegetable, 0 fruit, 3 bread, 0 meat, 0 fat*

OUT TO LUNCH

When it comes to having takeout, it's what you eat *with* the meal that makes a difference. If you're eating only pizza, it's easy to gobble down three or four slices. But round out your meal with a quick homemade salad, and you'll eat less.

For Chinese food, transfer it from the paper container to a plate, leaving extra sauce (and calories) behind. Ask if you can get brown rice instead of white for extra fiber.

And rather than filling your plate with too much of one thing, you're better off getting four $\frac{1}{2}$-cup portions of everything you want at a place like Boston Market, even if that includes a fattening dish such as stuffing. That way, you'll get a more appetizing variety of colors, nutrients, and calories.

Susan's Sweet 'n' Spicy Tomato-Basil Pasta

—Susan Howle, Columbia, South Carolina

"I have found that the sweet-spicy taste of this sauce leaves my tastebuds feeling quite satisfied. I serve this dish with a fresh garden salad."

2 cans (14½ ounces each) petite diced tomatoes

2 tablespoons sugar

2 large cloves garlic, minced

2 tablespoons dried basil

Pinch of dried oregano

Pinch of red-pepper flakes

1 tablespoon balsamic vinegar

1 teaspoon olive oil

Dry red wine to taste

12 ounces linguine or fettuccine

Grated Parmesan cheese

In a large saucepan over medium-high heat, combine the tomatoes, sugar, garlic, basil, oregano, red-pepper flakes, vinegar, oil, and wine. Cover and cook for 20 minutes, or until reduced and the flavors have blended.

Meanwhile, prepare the pasta according to package directions. Serve the sauce over the pasta and sprinkle with the cheese.

Makes 6 servings

Per serving: *266 calories, 9 g protein, 55 g carbohydrates, 2 g fat, 0 mg cholesterol, 180 mg sodium, 5 g dietary fiber*

Diet Exchanges: *0 milk, 1½ vegetable, 0 fruit, 3 bread, 0 meat, 0 fat*

Rotini with Roasted Vegetable Sauce

439 Calories

1 **red bell pepper, cut into 1" pieces**
1 **medium sweet potato, peeled and cut into ½" pieces**
½ **medium butternut squash, peeled and cut into ½" pieces**
½ **medium eggplant, cut into 1" pieces**
3 **portobello mushrooms, thickly sliced**
   Salt and black pepper
1 **bulb garlic**
2 **pounds plum tomatoes, halved lengthwise**
1 **can (15 ounces) tomato sauce**
8 **ounces tricolor rotini**
¼ **cup finely chopped fresh basil**
2 **tablespoons toasted pine nuts**

Preheat the oven to 400°F. Coat 2 baking sheets with cooking spray.

Place the bell pepper, sweet potato, squash, eggplant, and mushrooms on one of the baking sheets and mist with cooking spray. Sprinkle lightly with salt and black pepper.

Slice ¼" off the top of the garlic bulb and discard. Set the bulb on a piece of foil and wrap loosely. Place on the second baking sheet.

Squeeze each tomato half to remove the seeds and excess juice. Place the tomatoes, cut side up, on the sheet with the garlic. Mist with cooking spray and sprinkle lightly with salt and black pepper. Place both sheets in the oven. Bake for 25 minutes. Remove the

tomatoes and garlic from the oven. Bake the vegetables for 10 to 15 minutes longer, or until lightly browned and softened.

Place the tomatoes and other vegetables in a large saucepan. Stir in the tomato sauce. Squeeze the garlic cloves from their skins into a small bowl. Mash into a paste and stir into the sauce. Simmer for 15 minutes.

Meanwhile, prepare the pasta according to package directions. Add to the saucepan and toss to coat. Serve sprinkled with the basil and pine nuts.

Makes 4 servings

Per serving: *439 calories, 16 g protein, 89 g carbohydrates, 5 g fat, 0 mg cholesterol, 680 mg sodium, 12 g dietary fiber*

Diet Exchanges: *0 milk, 5 ;1/2 vegetable, 0 fruit, 4 bread, 0 meat, ½ fat*

Kitchen Tip

The sauce can be made up to 2 days in advance. To reheat, stir in about ¼ cup water and place over low heat for 10 minutes, or until hot. You can roast or steam the unused squash and eggplant to serve alongside any lean red meat, poultry, or fish.

Fiery Fusilli

389 Calories

8 ounces fusilli

1 tablespoon olive oil

1 clove garlic, minced

2 banana chile peppers, minced (wear plastic gloves when handling)

4 plum tomatoes, chopped

1 large roasted red pepper, chopped

2 tablespoons chopped Italian parsley

1 tablespoon chopped fresh sage

2 teaspoons chopped fresh oregano

1/8 teaspoon salt

1 can (14–19 ounces) chickpeas, rinsed and drained

1/2 cup fat-free chicken broth

1/4 teaspoon crushed red-pepper flakes

Prepare the pasta according to the package directions. Drain and place in a serving bowl.

Meanwhile, heat the oil in a large nonstick skillet over medium-high heat. Add the garlic and chile peppers and cook for 2 minutes, or until the peppers are tender. Add the tomatoes, roasted pepper, parsley, sage, oregano, and salt and cook for 5 minutes, or until the tomatoes begin to release their juice. Add the chickpeas, broth, and red-pepper flakes and cook for 2 minutes. Pour the sauce over the pasta and toss to combine.

Makes 4 servings

Per serving: *389 calories, 15 g protein, 71 g carbohydrates, 6 g fat, 0 mg cholesterol, 420 mg sodium, 8 g dietary fiber*

Diet Exchanges: *0 milk, 1 1/2 vegetable, 0 fruit, 4 1/2 bread, 0 meat, 1/2 fat*

Great-Tasting Good 4 U Breakfast

—Sally Fisher, Alva, Florida

"I eat this about five times a week, and it keeps me satisfied for many hours. If you like crunchy cereal, just add it a little at a time to the yogurt and don't stir. If you don't like your cereal crunchy, just stir all of it into the yogurt and enjoy."

1 **cup fat-free plain yogurt**
½ **cup fresh or frozen and thawed blueberries**
½ **cup fresh or frozen and thawed strawberries, halved**
½ **teaspoon vanilla extract**
¾ **cup whole grain cereal**

In a small bowl, combine the yogurt, blueberries, strawberries, and vanilla extract. Sprinkle the cereal over the top.

Makes 1 serving

Per serving: *270 calories, 14 g protein, 59 g carbohydrates, 2 g fat, 5 mg cholesterol, 210 mg sodium, 12 g dietary fiber*

Diet Exchanges: *1 milk, 0 vegetable, 1 fruit, 0 bread, 0 meat, 0 fat*

Kitchen Tip

This also makes a wonderful dessert. Just substitute frozen yogurt for regular, and you have a crunchy, fruity sundae.

BREAKFAST FOR LUNCH

Researchers at Purdue University had 28 people eat cereal with ⅔ cup of fat-free milk and a piece of fruit for two meals each day (breakfast and either lunch or dinner). The "breakfast club" also snacked on fruits and veggies and ate a normal third meal. After 2 weeks on the twice-a-day cereal diet, the average weight loss was 4.2 pounds. Because cereal is also a great way to get diet-enhancing fiber, be sure to choose one that contains at least 7 grams of fiber per serving.

229 Calories

Apple-Cinnamon Yogurt

—Marci Herman, Burnaby, British Columbia

"This recipe has been a godsend for me, and it takes only about 2 minutes to prepare. It's very satisfying and keeps you feeling full for several hours. It's the perfect breakfast to take to work and a great midafternoon snack when I get the munchies."

1 small apple, cored and chopped
2 tablespoons chopped walnuts
1 teaspoon honey (optional)
⅛ teaspoon ground cinnamon
½ cup fat-free plain yogurt

Place the apple and walnuts in a microwaveable bowl. Top with the honey, if using, and cinnamon. Microwave on high power for 1 minute, or until warmed. Top with the yogurt.

Makes 1 serving

Per serving: *229 calories, 7 g protein, 34 g carbohydrates, 10 g fat, 5 mg cholesterol, 70 mg sodium, 6 g dietary fiber*

Diet Exchanges: *½ milk, 0 vegetable, 1½ fruit, 0 bread, ½ meat, 1½ fat*

SHOPPING SAVVY

Super Cereal

The more fiber in your food, the fuller you feel. That's where this lightly sweetened combo of flax, bran flakes, Kamut puffs, and soy comes in. Optimum by Nature's Path is a high-fiber (10 grams per serving!) blueberry-flavored cereal that tastes great and gets your day started right. Plus, there are only 2.5 grams of fat and 190 calories per 1-cup serving. Look for it in natural food stores and many supermarkets.

Quick and Healthy Oatmeal

—Natasha Marchewka, Folsom, California

"This recipe is filling, nutritionally balanced, and full of fiber, so it keeps my hunger at bay with no need to eat for hours. The soy milk and syrup make it especially rich and satisfying."

1 **cup soy milk or water**
½ **cup old-fashioned oats**
¼ **cup blueberries or raspberries**
1 **tablespoon maple syrup**

Combine the milk or water and oats in a medium saucepan over medium-high heat and bring to a boil. (Use more or less liquid to reach desired consistency.) Reduce the heat to low and simmer for 5 minutes.

Serve topped with the berries and maple syrup.

Makes 1 serving

Per serving: *300 calories, 12 g protein, 50 g carbohydrates, 8 g fat, 0 mg cholesterol, 35 mg sodium, 8 g dietary fiber*

Diet Exchanges: *0 milk, 0 vegetable, ½ fruit, 3 bread, ½ meat, 1 fat*

LOSE WEIGHT WITH LOTS OF FIBER

When researchers looked at the lifestyles of nearly 13,000 middle-aged men from seven countries, they discovered that fiber—not fat—determined how trim they were.

The diets of the leanest men featured a whopping 40 percent fat, but they also averaged 41 grams fiber a day. Dietary fat can make you fat, because it has lots of calories, but fiber may cancel out some of those calories, explains study author Daan Kromhout, Ph.D., of the National Institute of Public Health and Environment in the Netherlands.

Fiber-rich foods can actually whisk some calories out of your body before they end up on your hips. Plus, fiber fills you up for fewer calories, so you eat less overall. When you do eat fat, make sure it's the good-for-you monounsaturated kind found in avocados, nuts, and olive oil. Then increase your fiber to at least 25 to 35 grams daily.

Some good high-fiber choices:

1 cup baked acorn squash: 10 grams

1 cup black bean soup: 10 grams

4 fresh figs: 6.5 grams

1 cup hot multigrain cereal: 5 grams

1 large baked apple: 5 grams

1 large pear: 5 grams

¼ cup roasted pumpkin seeds: 5 grams

It Worked for Me!

Millie Wiley

An ultra low-fat approach helped Millie lose weight without counting calories. For maintenance, she still eats a low-fat diet overall but is careful not to binge on too many fat-free processed foods.

"I was 47 when my husband and I retired to settle into a quiet life in rural Virginia. It was at that same time that I noticed the pounds that had started settling onto me. From being thin nearly all my life, I had gained 40 pounds in about 10 years.

"Things got worse when I was diagnosed with breast cancer, and the chemotherapy caused me to gain weight. Before I knew it, my weight had soared to 181 pounds.

"I finally looked at myself one day, and just knew it: I was fat, and I had to do something about it.

"I had a doctor's appointment that month, and it turns out, my doctor's practice had just contracted with a nutritionist. I made an appointment, and the nutritionist measured my body fat and hydration levels—both rated 'poor.' She counseled me on the importance of eating less fat, drinking more water, and getting exercise.

"Her advice sounded simple. I started watching my fat intake and began taking a daily multivitamin. I also really took to the drinking rule. I kept a 16-ounce glass on my kitchen counter and set a goal of 10 cups a day. My complexion improved and I also noticed that I got fewer colds.

"The bigger challenge was exercise—the word alone was enough to make me cringe. But when a friend loaned me a walking tape, I was surprised to find I loved it. I looked forward to my walks, which took me around the neighborhood for 45 minutes at a time, four times a week. It's still my favorite way to start the day.

"All this time, I avoided hamburgers, cheese, mayonnaise, butter, nuts, and desserts (except for the fat-free kind). I didn't count calories—I just ate healthier. I devoured fruits and vegetables and used smart substitutions like butter spray and fat-free sour cream.

"In 9 months, I was down to 130 pounds and could fit into a size 8. Today, my blood pressure is back to normal and a recent bone density test shows that a weak spot I once had has improved, thanks to the bone-strengthening effects of walking. I'm also happy to say that I remain cancer-free."

Garden Bounty Omelets

190 Calories

3 plum tomatoes, chopped

2 scallions, chopped

1 red bell pepper, chopped

¼ cup chopped fresh dill

4 egg whites

2 eggs

2 teaspoons fat-free milk

Salt and black pepper

4 tablespoons shredded reduced-fat smoked Jarlsberg cheese

Heat a medium nonstick skillet coated with cooking spray over medium heat. Add the tomatoes, scallions, bell pepper, and dill and cook, stirring frequently, for 7 minutes, or until soft. Place the vegetables in a small bowl. Wipe out the skillet and recoat with cooking spray. Return to the heat.

In a medium bowl, whisk together the egg whites, eggs, and milk. Season with the salt and black pepper. Pour half of the egg mixture into the skillet and cook, occasionally scraping the bottom of the pan, for 2 minutes. Sprinkle half of the vegetable mixture over the eggs and top with 2 tablespoons of the cheese. Cook for 3 minutes, or until the cheese is melted, the bottom is golden brown, and the eggs are set.

Using a large spatula, flip the omelet in half, remove to a plate, and keep warm. Recoat the skillet with cooking spray. Repeat with the remaining egg mixture, vegetables, and cheese to make another omelet.

Makes 2 omelets

Per omelet: *190 calories, 20 g protein, 11 g carbohydrates, 7 g fat, 255 mg cholesterol, 630 mg sodium, 2 g dietary fiber*

Diet Exchanges: *0 milk, 1½ vegetable, 0 fruit, 0 bread, 2½ meat, ½ fat*

MEASURE CEREAL AND LOSE 10 POUNDS

Allowed to eyeball their portions in a study, adults helped themselves to twice the 1-cup serving of whole wheat flakes recommended on the box. Simply cutting back to the recommended 1-cup serving would save more than 36,500 calories a year—a 10-pound weight loss.

Hearty Waffles

—Lorie Prouty, San José, California

"This is a delicious, high-fiber, hearty meal that keeps me satisfied for hours until lunch. It also satisfies my sweet tooth so I'm not tempted by midmorning snacks."

½ cup quick-cooking oatmeal

¼ cup oat bran

2 tablespoons whole wheat flour

2 tablespoons unbleached all-purpose flour

1½ tablespoons packed brown sugar

1 tablespoon ground cinnamon

½ teaspoon ground nutmeg

1¼ cups fat-free milk

1 tablespoon canola oil

2 tablespoons lite blueberry or maple syrup

½ cup blueberries

In a large bowl, combine the oatmeal, oat bran, whole wheat flour, all-purpose flour, brown sugar, cinnamon, and nutmeg. Add the milk and oil and stir to combine. Refrigerate for 30 minutes, or until the batter is thickened.

Preheat a waffle iron according to the manufacturer's directions. Pour the batter onto the waffle iron (amount will vary according to manufacturer) and cook for 5 minutes, or until golden brown. Serve topped with the syrup and blueberries.

Makes 2 waffles

Per waffle: *370 calories, 13 g protein, 64 g carbohydrates, 10 g fat, 5 mg cholesterol, 290 mg sodium, 8 g dietary fiber*

Diet Exchanges: *½ milk, 0 vegetable, ½ fruit, 3 bread, 0 meat, ½ fat*

HEALTHY "JUNK FOOD"

If quick and convenient junk food is your weakness, have no fear. All you need to do is make a few better choices. Select "healthier" junk foods such as flavored oatmeal instead of sugary cereals, a burrito instead of a hot dog, or toasted pita crisps and hummus instead of potato chips and dip.

And avoid starting your day with a doughnut or pastry. These sugary treats can leave you feeling hungry again very quickly. If you absolutely must have one, consider it a special treat, and pair your goodie with a healthy food such as an apple to help you ward off the munchies later on.

Cinnamon Chip Muffins

—Nancy J. Dornette, Cincinnati

"I enjoy one of these muffins for breakfast along with a half of a grapefruit and a cup of coffee. It satisfies my sweet tooth without being too sweet or loaded with fat."

1	tablespoon cinnamon sugar
1½	cups unbleached all-purpose flour
½	cup sugar
3	teaspoons baking powder
½	teaspoon salt
½	cup fat-free milk
1	egg, lightly beaten
¼	cup light butter or margarine, melted
3	ounces cinnamon baking chips

Preheat the oven to 400°F. Line a 12-cup muffin pan with paper liners. Dust the bottoms with the cinnamon sugar.

In a large bowl, combine the flour, sugar, baking powder, and salt. Add the milk, egg, and butter and stir until just combined. Stir in the cinnamon chips. Evenly divide the batter among the muffin cups.

Bake for 20 minutes, or until a wooden pick inserted in the center of a muffin comes out clean.

Makes 12 muffins

Per muffin: *157 calories, 3 g protein, 26 g carbohydrates, 5 g fat, 30 mg cholesterol, 260 mg sodium, 1 g dietary fiber*

Diet Exchanges: *0 milk, 0 vegetable, 0 fruit, 1½ bread, 0 meat, 1 fat*

BREAD & BREAKFAST

The right slice of bread could help you trim extra weight. In an Australian study, participants ate different breads on separate mornings, then rated their feelings of hunger and fullness for 2 hours. Compared with a popular American white bread, the top choices rated up to five times more satisfying and caused subjects to eat less the rest of the day. The best slices were crunchy, chewy, and filling.

A coarse texture activates more sensory receptors in your mouth and takes longer to eat, so you realize as soon as you're getting full. Plus, grainy bread is digested more slowly, so you stay satisfied longer.

Check labels to be sure each slice contains 3 to 5 grams of fiber. Also, the word "whole" should appear first in the ingredients list.

The most slimming slices: 100 percent stone-ground whole wheat, whole grain pitas and bagels, whole grain fruit (such as raisin), and whole grain sourdough and European-style rye (made from whole kernel rye).

My Bran Muffins

—Patti Bauml, Duncan, British Columbia

" I have two small boys, and I do not have a lot of time in the morning to eat a regular meal. So I grab one of these muffins on the way out the door to take the kids to school. "

2 cups high-fiber cereal, such as All-Bran

1½ cups water

¼ cup unsweetened applesauce

2 egg whites

¾ cup whole wheat flour

½ cup bran

1 tablespoon artificial sweetener, such as Sweet 'N Low

1½ teaspoons baking powder

1 teaspoon ground cinnamon

½ teaspoon ground nutmeg

½ teaspoon cloves

½ teaspoon baking soda

Preheat the oven to 350°F. Coat a 12-cup muffin pan with cooking spray.

In a medium bowl, combine the cereal and water and let stand for 2 minutes. Add the applesauce and egg whites and stir to mix.

In another medium bowl, combine the flour, bran, sweetener, baking powder, cinnamon, nutmeg, cloves, and baking soda. Add the applesauce mixture and stir until just combined. Evenly divide the batter among the muffin cups.

Bake for 20 minutes, or until a wooden pick inserted in the center of a muffin comes out clean.

Makes 12 muffins

Per muffin: *70 calories, 3 g protein, 16 g carbohydrates, 1 g fat, 0 mg cholesterol, 210 mg sodium, 6 g dietary fiber*

Diet Exchanges: *0 milk, 0 vegetable, 0 fruit, ½ bread, 0 meat, 0 fat*

Cranberry Bread

—Anne Brown, Denton, Texas

"This is the best recipe for giving a satisfying sweet end to a light meal, particularly if you like cinnamon. Wrapped in foil, the bread will keep for about a week. When heated in the microwave, it tastes freshly baked."

1½ **cups whole wheat flour**

½ **cup unbleached all-purpose flour**

⅔ **cup sugar**

1 **teaspoon salt**

1 **teaspoon ground cinnamon**

½ **teaspoon baking soda**

1 **large egg**

1 **can (16 ounces) whole-berry cranberry sauce**

1 **cup chopped walnuts**

Preheat the oven to 350°F. Coat a loaf pan with cooking spray.

In a large bowl, combine the whole wheat flour, all-purpose flour, sugar, salt, cinnamon, and baking soda. Add the egg, cranberry sauce, and walnuts and mix just until moistened (the mixture will be dry and take effort to mix). Pour into the prepared loaf pan.

Bake for 1 hour, or until a wooden pick inserted in the center comes out clean. Cool for 10 minutes in the pan. Remove to a rack and cool completely.

Makes 12 servings

Per serving: *287 calories, 6 g protein, 50 g carbohydrates, 9 g fat, 21 mg cholesterol, 313 mg sodium, 4 g dietary fiber*

Diet Exchanges: *0 milk, 0 vegetable, 1 fruit, 2 bread, 0 meat, 1½ fat*

Quick Cinnamon Rolls

212 Calories

½ cup packed light brown sugar

½ cup raisins, finely chopped

3 tablespoons wheat-and-barley nuggets cereal, such as Grape-Nuts

2 tablespoons finely chopped toasted walnuts

2 teaspoons ground cinnamon

2 tubes (11 ounces each) refrigerated bread dough

1 tablespoon + 1½ teaspoons butter or margarine, melted

1 egg white, lightly beaten with 1 tablespoon water

⅓ cup confectioners' sugar

1 tablespoon fat-free milk

½ teaspoon vanilla extract

Preheat the oven to 375°F. Lightly coat a 13" × 9" baking dish with cooking spray.

In a medium bowl, combine the brown sugar, raisins, cereal, walnuts, and cinnamon. Unroll the dough on a lightly floured surface. Place 1 piece on top of the other. Pinch the edges to seal. Roll into an 18" × 12" rectangle. Brush the surface with 1 tablespoon of the butter or margarine. Sprinkle evenly with the brown sugar mixture, pressing the filling lightly into the dough. Starting with a long side, roll the dough into a tube, brushing the outside of the dough with egg white as you roll. Pinch the seam to seal. Cut into 12 slices and place the slices, cut side up, in the prepared baking dish. Brush the tops with the remaining 1½ teaspoons butter or margarine.

Bake for 18 to 20 minutes, or until golden brown. Remove to a rack to cool slightly.

Meanwhile, in a small bowl, combine the confectioners' sugar, milk, and vanilla extract. Drizzle over the rolls.

Makes 12 rolls

Per roll: *212 calories, 6 g protein, 39 g carbohydrates, 5 g fat, 5 mg cholesterol, 310 mg sodium, 2 g dietary fiber*

Diet Exchanges: *0 milk, 0 vegetable, ½ fruit, 2 bread, 0 meat, ½ fat*

Easy Entertaining

Shakes and Smoothies

Dips, Pizzas, and Tortillas

Grills, Casseroles, and Chilis

Yogurt-Berry Smoothie

185 Calories

—Susan Lewen, Spring Valley, California

"This low-fat, low-calorie treat helps fulfill your fruit requirement for the day."

1 cup frozen berries, such as blueberries, raspberries, or strawberries

½ cup low-fat yogurt (any flavor)

½ cup orange juice or other juice

Place the berries, yogurt, and orange juice in a blender and pulse for 30 seconds. Blend for 30 seconds, or until smooth.

Makes 1 serving

Per serving: *185 calories, 8 g protein, 35 g carbohydrates, 2 g fat, 7 mg cholesterol, 90 mg sodium, 3 g dietary fiber*

Diet Exchanges: *1 milk, 0 vegetable, 2 fruit, 0 bread, 0 meat, 0 fat*

Mixed Fruit Slush

125 Calories

—Mildred Kihn, Sacramento

"I have this for breakfast every day. It gives me my morning start and helps carry me over until lunch."

1 can (20 ounces) unsweetened pineapple chunks, drained

1 can (15 ounces) mixed fruit, such as peaches, pears, pineapples, and grapes, drained

1 cup frozen strawberries

1 medium banana

In a blender, combine the pineapple, mixed fruit, strawberries, and banana and blend until smooth.

Makes 4 servings

Per serving: *125 calories, 1 g protein, 33 g carbohydrates, 0 g fat, 0 mg cholesterol, 10 mg sodium, 4 g dietary fiber*

Diet Exchanges: *0 milk, 0 vegetable, 2 fruit, 0 bread, 0 meat, 0 fat*

Kitchen Tip

If you prefer a thinner shake, just add a little of the liquid from the canned fruit to the blender before processing. For added chill in the summertime, add ½ cup crushed ice to the mix and pulse once or twice in the blender.

Banana-Berry Smoothie

—Natasha Marchewka, Folsom, California

"This recipe fills me up for breakfast or a snack and quells my need for sweets."

1 **cup orange juice**
½ **cup plain or vanilla soy milk**
½ **banana**
¾ **cup frozen mixed berries**

In a blender, combine the orange juice, milk, banana, and berries and blend until smooth.

Makes 2 servings

Per serving: *181 calories, 3 g protein, 41 g carbohydrates, 2 g fat, 0 mg cholesterol, 10 mg sodium, 5 g dietary fiber*

Diet Exchanges: *0 milk, 0 vegetable, 3 fruit, 0 bread, 0 meat, 0 fat*

SHOPPING SAVVY

A Cuppa Soy

If chocolate is your weakness and you're trying to lose weight, a steaming cup of hot cocoa can satisfy your craving. Country Choice Naturals instant hot cocoa mixes give you a rich, chocolatey flavor that's certified organic, with no refined sweeteners, hydrogenated oils, or artificial colors or flavors. Try Royal Chocolate, Irish Chocolate Mint, Chocolate Orange Cream, or Chocolate Cinnamon Spice for only 1 gram of fat and 100 calories per serving. They're available in natural food stores and some larger supermarkets, or visit their Web site at www.countrychoicenaturals.com.

My Favorite Smoothie

—Tina LaBrie, Estes Park, Colorado

"I've found that smoothies are great for an after-workout treat. They fill me up with nutritious, great-tasting, energizing calories, so I can stay away from junk food."

1 cup vanilla soy milk

½ cup frozen fruit, such as blueberries, strawberries, and raspberries

½ cup low-fat or fat-free vanilla soy or dairy yogurt

2 tablespoons soy protein powder (optional)

2 tablespoons ground flax seeds (optional)

In a blender, combine the milk, fruit, and yogurt and blend well. Add the protein powder, if using, and flax seeds, if using, and blend well.

Makes 2 servings

Per serving: *149 calories, 6 g protein, 25 g carbohydrates, 4 g fat, 0 mg cholesterol, 53 mg sodium, 1 g dietary fiber*

Diet Exchanges: *0 milk, 2 vegetable, 1 fruit, ½ bread, 0 meat, ½ fat*

Orange Skimsicle

—Julie Deel, Selbyville, Delaware

"This was my first quickie shake creation. It's perfect for a snack after a workout or for breakfast."

½ cup low-fat vanilla ice cream or frozen yogurt, softened

¼ cup frozen orange juice concentrate

3–4 ice cubes

In a blender, combine the ice cream or yogurt, orange juice, and ice cubes. Blend until smooth. Serve in a freezer-chilled glass.

Makes 1 serving

Per serving: *155 calories, 4 g protein, 30 g carbohydrates, 2 g fat, 5 mg cholesterol, 50 mg sodium, 1 g dietary fiber*

Diet Exchanges: *0 milk, 0 vegetable, 1 fruit, 1 bread, 0 meat, 1 fat*

Chocolate–Peanut Butter Shake

280 Calories

—Cynthia Dale, Lancaster, Pennsylvania

"I peel and freeze overripe bananas to keep on hand for fruit smoothies and these shakes. When using a frozen banana in the recipe, I use only 6 ice cubes."

2 cups cold chocolate soy milk

1 teaspoon vanilla extract

1 large banana

2 tablespoons creamy reduced-fat peanut butter

6–8 ice cubes

Makes 2 servings

Per serving: *280 calories, 9 g protein, 46 g carbohydrates, 8 g fat, 0 mg cholesterol, 220 mg sodium, 3 g dietary fiber*

Diet Exchanges: *0 milk, 5 vegetable, 1 fruit, 0 bread, 0 meat, 1 fat*

In a blender, combine the milk, vanilla extract, banana, peanut butter, and ice cubes and process until thick and smooth.

SECRETS OF WEIGHT-LOSS WINNERS

• I make weight training a nonnegotiable, essential part of my routine.

—Debra Herbst, Gig Harbor, Washington

• Taking a Spinning class really hooked me on exercise. Later, I added step aerobics and weight lifting. It became easy to make the time to exercise because I actually looked forward to it.

—Susan Glazer, Langhorne, Pennsylvania

• While you are watching TV, make sure you move. You can do light leg lifts, arm exercises with water-filled pop bottles, and arm stretches over your head. The point is to just move and keep your heart rate up a bit.

—Barbara Meyers, Oregon, Ohio

Fizzy Grapefruit

—Julie Deel, Selbyville, Delaware

" This is one of my favorite summer drinks. Whipping the air into it with the blender fills you up fast and makes you full without consuming a lot of calories. "

½ **pink grapefruit**
1 **cup lite pink lemonade**
3–4 **ice cubes**

Scoop the pulp out of the grapefruit halves and place in a blender. Squeeze any remaining juice from the grapefruit halves into the blender. Add the lemonade and ice cubes and blend until smooth. Serve in a freezer-chilled glass.

Makes 1 serving

Per serving: *21 calories, 0 g protein, 5 g carbohydrates, 0 g fat, 0 mg cholesterol, 1 mg sodium, 1 g dietary fiber*

Diet Exchanges: *0 milk, 0 vegetable, ½ fruit, 0 bread, 0 meat, 0 fat*

SNACK SWAPS

If you like sweet snacks, here are a few smart swaps so you can get your fill without gaining weight.

- Instead of Snickers (2.07 ounces, 280 calories), choose Milky Way Lite (1.57 ounces, 170 calories); save 110 calories.
- Instead of 2 chocolate chip cookies (2½ inches diameter, 280 calories), choose 2 sugar cookies (2½ inches diameter, 130 calories); save 150 calories.
- Instead of 20 Peanut M&Ms (202 calories), choose 20 Plain M&Ms (68 calories); save 134 calories.
- Instead of ½ cup Häagen-Dazs chocolate ice cream (270 calories), choose ½ cup Breyers chocolate ice cream (160 calories); save 110 calories.

Roasted Veggie Dip

—Jan Bell, Fort Wayne, Indiana

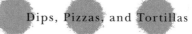

6 Calories

"This recipe is so easy as well as great tasting. I found this was a great way for me to eat my veggies while I was focusing on eating right in an effort to lose weight."

1 **medium yellow squash**
1 **bell pepper, any color**
1 **red onion**
1 **medium zucchini**
1 **cucumber, halved and seeded**
2 **cloves garlic, minced**
¼ **teaspoon salt**
¼ **teaspoon black or red pepper**
1 **tablespoon tomato paste**
   Baked pita crisps, crudités, or baked tortilla chips

Preheat the oven to 400°F. Coat a jelly-roll pan or large baking pan with cooking spray.

Cut the squash, bell pepper, onion, zucchini, and cucumber into large chunks. Place on the prepared baking sheet and coat with cooking spray. Sprinkle with the garlic, salt, and pepper. Bake for 30 minutes, turning once, or until the vegetables are tender and lightly browned.

Place in a blender or food processor. Add the tomato paste and puree until just blended, but with some texture. Remove to a serving bowl and serve warm or cold with the crisps, crudités, or chips.

Makes 24 servings (2 tablespoons each)

Per 2 tablespoons: *6 calories, 0 g protein, 1 g carbohydrates, 0 g fat, 0 mg cholesterol, 25 mg sodium, 0 g dietary fiber*

Diet Exchanges: *0 milk, 0 vegetable, 0 fruit, 0 bread, 0 meat, 0 fat*

Kitchen Tip

This dip can also be frozen, so when company arrives, you'll have a great-tasting appetizer to serve.

Vegetable Dill Dip

—Jennie Lynn Larson, Madison, Wisconsin

21 Calories

"I like to serve this dip with vegetable sticks, low-fat crackers, or baked corn chips."

⅔ **cup cottage cheese**
4 **tablespoons low-fat mayonnaise**
1 **tablespoon fat-free milk**
1 **tablespoon lemon juice**
1 **tablespoon onion flakes**
1 **teaspoon garlic salt**
1 **teaspoon dried dill**

In a blender, combine the cottage cheese, mayonnaise, milk, lemon juice, onion flakes, garlic salt, and dill. Blend until just smooth.

Makes 16 servings (1 tablespoon each)

Per tablespoon: *21 calories, 1 g protein, 1 g carbohydrates, 1 g fat, 2 mg cholesterol, 129 mg sodium, 1 g dietary fiber*

Diet Exchanges: *0 milk, 0 vegetable, 0 fruit, 0 bread, 0 meat, ½ fat*

SHOPPING SAVVY

A Zesty Spread

Low fat equals high flavor when you let zesty mustard do the honors. Spread it on sandwiches instead of mayo and save a ton of fat. Or use it (alone or mixed with yogurt) as a dip for vegetables, shrimp, pretzels, and more. For a host of unusual varieties, see the mustards from Terrapin Ridge. Among the gourmet choices are Sweet Beet and Horseradish, Thai Curry and Sweet Basil, Wasabi Lime, Smokey Onion, and Orange Cranberry. Look for the mustard at Crate and Barrel, Whole Foods, and specialty stores or visit www.terrapinridge.com.

All-Purpose Garlic Dip

—Valerie Veilleux, Orleans, Ontario

"You can add chili powder, Cajun mix, onion powder, Italian seasoning, dill, lemon pepper, or anything else you like to this dip. You can also spread it on chicken and coat with crushed cereal, then bake. Or, spread it on fish, wrap in foil, and cook on the barbecue."

1 bulb garlic
⅓ cup reduced-fat cream cheese, softened
⅓ cup low-fat mayonnaise
⅓ cup fat-free plain yogurt

Preheat the oven to 350°F.

Place the garlic bulb on a piece of foil, moisten with water, and seal. Bake for 45 minutes. When cool enough to handle, squeeze the garlic from the bulb.

In a small bowl, combine the garlic, cream cheese, mayonnaise, and yogurt. Stir until smooth.

Makes 8 servings (2 tablespoons each)

Per 2 tablespoons: *53 calories, 2 g protein, 4 g carbohydrates, 4 g fat, 10 mg cholesterol, 85 mg sodium, 0 g dietary fiber*

Diet Exchanges: *0 milk, 0 vegetable, 0 fruit, 0 bread, 0 meat, ½ fat*

Hummus Salad

18 Calories

—Renée Rewiski, Hawthorne, New Jersey

"I eat this for lunch, or even after my evening yoga class as a light dinner.
It's filling, tasty, and leaves me with no cravings."

2 large carrots, chopped
2 tablespoons water
6 black olives, chopped
1 scallion, chopped
1 can (15 ounces) chickpeas
1 clove garlic
1 tablespoon grapeseed oil or other oil
Pinch of salt

Place the carrots and water in a microwave-able bowl. Cover with plastic wrap and microwave for 4 minutes, or until tender-crisp. Drain. Add the olives and scallion.

In a food processor or blender, combine the chickpeas, garlic, and oil until almost a smooth paste. Add to the carrot mixture and sprinkle with the salt. Stir to combine.

Makes 40 servings (1 tablespoon each)

Per Tablespoon: *18 calories, 1 g protein, 3 g carbohydrates, 1 g fat, 0 mg cholesterol, 46 mg sodium, 1 g dietary fiber*

Diet Exchanges: *0 milk, ½ vegetable, 0 fruit, ½ bread, 0 meat, 0 fat*

Kitchen Tip

This tasty hummus is terrific served with celery or carrot sticks, rice cakes, or your favorite crackers.

SHOPPING SAVVY

A Chip off the Old . . . Carrot

Carrot Chips are diagonal slices of mature carrots shaped like potato chips and perfect for scooping. An entire 16-ounce bag (2½ cups) has only 190 calories and no fat. That's about the same amount of calories in only 1 ounce of potato chips. With the beta-carotene, potassium, and fiber that fresh carrots provide, it's a switch that makes good nutritional sense. Look for Carrot Chips from Grimmway Farms in the produce section or visit their Web site at www.grimmway.com.

It Worked for Me!

Ron Burke

VITAL STATS

Weight lost: 26 pounds

Time to goal: 6 months

Unique secret to success:
Keeping an optimistic attitude let each small success become an incentive for the next one

*A*ddictions brought Ron's health to rock bottom and his weight to an all-time high. He kicked the habits and lost the weight, boosting both his health and his self-confidence.

"An aneurysm in my leg was causing poor circulation and ulcers that now required treatment. My doctor told me I had a fifty-fifty chance of losing my leg. If I had taken better care of myself, my situation wouldn't have come to this, but I was an addict. My weakness for drugs and alcohol had worsened over the years until I hit this low point.

"When I first started having problems with my leg, I took advantage of it. I lived off disability and spent most of my time feeling sorry for myself—and eating. Cake, candy bars, and potato chips were my staples. I seldom ate actual meals, and when I did, it was a bowl of sugary cereal or a fast-food burger and fries.

"By the time I checked in to the hospital for my leg, I had also developed high blood pressure. Before operating, the surgeon asked if he could pray for me. This kind gesture finally hit me: I could actually die.

"The operation saved my leg and kept me in the hospital for just enough time to get

the drugs out of my system. I started reading spiritual and self-help books. When I left the hospital, I joined Alcoholics Anonymous. I decided to start walking, despite the fact that the operation had left me with a limp.

"I worked up to walking 1 mile, then 2. I began to stretch and do crunches, jumping jacks, and push-ups. I also made it a point to start eating better.

"As my condition improved, so did my mind-set. I stopped feeling sorry for myself and got a job that I excelled at. Then I met my future wife, who became another incentive to take care of myself.

"I started going to a gym 5 days a week. My stress levels fell as my strength and endurance increased. And my diet got even better—after a hard workout, the last thing I wanted was a fattening meal. I preferred fruit, yogurt, or raw vegetables for breakfast or lunch. Dinner was grilled chicken and a salad.

"In 6 months, I lost 26 pounds, lowered my blood pressure, and was able to cut back on my medication. Today I am in the best shape of my life, and it's been more than 4 great years since I've had a drink or used drugs. If you believe in something enough, you can make it happen!"

Chicken Pesto Pizza

1 tablespoon cornmeal

1 tube (10 ounces) refrigerated pizza dough

⅓ cup low-fat prepared pesto

¼ pound cooked boneless, skinless chicken breast, cut into small strips

1 roasted red pepper, cut into small strips

½ cup rinsed and drained water-packed canned artichoke hearts, patted dry and quartered

½ cup (2 ounces) crumbled low-fat goat cheese or shredded low-fat Jarlsberg cheese

Preheat the oven to 450°F. Coat a large round pizza pan with cooking spray. Sprinkle with the cornmeal.

Turn the dough out onto a lightly floured work surface and roll into a 12" circle. Place on the prepared pan. Spread with the pesto, leaving a ¼" border, and top with the chicken, pepper strips, and artichokes. Dot with the goat cheese or sprinkle with Jarlsberg.

Bake for 10 minutes, or until the cheese is melted and the crust is golden brown.

Makes 8 servings

Per serving: *200 calories, 10 g protein, 20 g carbohydrates, 8 g fat, 15 mg cholesterol, 420 mg sodium, 1 g dietary fiber*

Diet Exchanges: *0 milk, ½ vegetable, 0 fruit, 1 bread, 1½ meat, 1 fat*

Mediterranean Pizza with Shrimp and Feta

174 Calories

2 tablespoons cornmeal

1 tube (10 ounces) refrigerated pizza dough

1 cup water

5 ounces large shrimp, peeled and deveined

1 tablespoon toasted pine nuts

1 large clove garlic

1½ cups loosely packed fresh basil

2 tablespoons grated Parmesan cheese

2–3 tablespoons fat-free chicken broth

2 teaspoons lemon juice

½ cup (2 ounces) crumbled feta cheese

2 tablespoons minced red onion

½ cup (2 ounces) shredded reduced-fat mozzarella cheese

Preheat the oven to 450°F. Coat a large round pizza pan with cooking spray. Sprinkle with the cornmeal.

Turn the dough out onto a lightly floured surface and role into a 12" circle.

Bring the water to a simmer in a small saucepan. Add the shrimp and cook for 2 minutes, or until opaque. Drain and cut each shrimp into thirds.

Place the pine nuts and garlic in a food processor or blender. Process until minced. Add the basil, Parmesan, broth, and lemon juice and process for 2 minutes, or until a paste forms. (Add more broth, if necessary, to achieve the desired consistency.) Spread the mixture on the crust, leaving a ½" border. Top with the shrimp, feta, onion, and mozzarella.

Bake for 14 minutes, or until the cheese is melted and the crust is golden brown.

Makes 8 servings

Per serving: *174 calories, 11 g protein, 20 g carbohydrates, 5 g fat, 40 mg cholesterol, 410 mg sodium, 1 g dietary fiber*

Diet Exchanges: *0 milk, 0 vegetable, 0 fruit, 1 bread, 1 meat, ½ fat*

Easy Chicken and Vegetable Pizza

—Robbin Jones, Fuquay Varina, North Carolina

"For a busy woman, this is an easy-to-prepare meal, and it has great flavor."

¼ cup prepared pesto
1 prebaked pizza shell
2 portobello mushrooms, sliced
1 yellow bell pepper, sliced
1 red bell pepper, sliced
½ red onion, sliced
1 Romano tomato, sliced
1 package (6 ounces) precooked Italian-flavor chicken strips
¼ cup (1 ounce) crumbled feta cheese
¼ cup (1 ounce) shredded Parmesan cheese
¼ cup (1 ounce) shredded mozzarella cheese

Preheat the oven to 375°F.

Using a pastry brush, brush the pesto onto the pizza shell. Top with the mushrooms, bell peppers, onion, tomato, chicken, feta, Parmesan, and mozzarella.

Bake for 20 minutes, or until the cheeses are melted and the crust is golden.

Makes 8 servings

Per serving: *321 calories, 21 g protein, 21 g carbohydrates, 18 g fat, 50 mg cholesterol, 450 mg sodium, 2 g dietary fiber*

Diet Exchanges: *Diet Exchanges: 0 milk, 0 fruit, 1½ vegetable, 1 bread, 2½ meat, 2½ fat*

Better Burritos

—Tina LaBrie, Estes Park, Colorado

"I found that adding a lot of flavor to my diet—spicy foods, for instance—helped me enjoy my diet so much more. When I enjoy the healthy foods I eat, I keep eating the foods my body needs, and that helps me lose weight."

4 **flour tortillas (8" in diameter)**

1 **can (14–19 ounces) vegetarian refried beans**

⅔ **cup salsa**

½ **cup (2 ounces) shredded Cheddar cheese**

½ **teaspoon ground cumin**

½ **teaspoon garlic powder**

Preheat the oven to 200°F.

Loosely wrap the tortillas in foil and warm in the oven for 10 minutes.

Meanwhile, heat a large skillet coated with cooking spray over low heat. Add the beans, ⅓ cup of the salsa, ¼ cup of the cheese, the cumin, and garlic powder and cook, stirring occasionally, for 8 minutes, or until cooked through and the cheese is melted.

Lay the tortillas on a work surface. Evenly divide the bean mixture among the tortillas. Fold in the sides of the tortillas and roll up from the bottom to enclose the filling. Top each burrito with the remaining salsa and cheese.

Makes 4 burritos

Per burrito: *273 calories, 13 g protein, 38 g carbohydrates, 8 g fat, 15 mg cholesterol, 990 mg sodium, 7 g dietary fiber*

Diet Exchanges: *0 milk, 1½ vegetable, 0 fruit, 2 bread, 1 meat, 1½ fat*

Kitchen Tip

Serve these burritos with a side salad of leafy greens and tomatoes topped with a low-fat ranch dressing.

It Worked for Me!

Lori LaRizzio

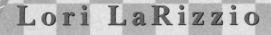

VITAL STATS

Weight lost: 60 pounds

Time to goal: 8 months

Unique secret to success: Making use of idle moments to fit mini-workouts into her day

Friends used to turn to Lori for her mouthwatering, fattening recipes. Lori has become such an example of healthy weight loss that now, friends come to her with questions about nutrition and exercise.

"As a licensed practical nurse, I should have been the picture of health. But my weight had been creeping steadily up since the birth of my first son 10 years ago, and my cholesterol was 259. My blood pressure was also too high, threatening me with hypertension.

"The problem didn't hit home until a friend asked me to be in her wedding. My sense of pride turned to horror when the salesperson at the bridal store told me I'd need to order a size 18 dress. I decided to do something about it immediately, so I ordered a size 16 instead and vowed to drop the extra pounds.

"My work schedule had included night and evening shifts, which bred poor eating habits that I was determined to break. I switched from sugary breakfast cereals to more satisfying, low-sugar Cheerios and fat-free milk. I snacked on fruit midmorning. And instead of a burger and fries for lunch, I

switched to a chicken or tuna sandwich with low-fat dressing.

"I also started bringing healthy frozen dinners to work, so I could avoid the fried chicken fingers and lemon meringue pie that normally seduced me in the hospital cafeteria. I'd pack apples or pretzels instead of grabbing cookies or buying candy.

"I started taking advantage of every possible free moment. If I had 20 minutes free over lunch, I'd ask a coworker to join me for a walk. Instead of sitting while waiting for my son during football practice, I'd take a quick stroll. If I found myself stuck at home on a rainy day, I'd pop in an exercise video or ride the stationary bike. Thanks to my mini-workouts, I have not missed a day of exercise since January 1997.

"I lost 10 pounds by the end of the first month. By the time my friend's wedding rolled around, I had to trade the size 16 dress in for a size 14, and it still needed to be taken in.

"Now, I find that I'm no longer tired all the time and I'm having fun. Most important, I've found that exercise is a wonderful social outlet, whether I'm walking with my husband or dancing with friends."

Black Bean Quesadillas

—Holly Kline, Cynthiana, Kentucky

"This recipe is extremely filling, so I often skip the sour cream and eat one quesadilla with a salad for a satisfying dinner."

1 can (14–19 ounces) no-salt black beans, rinsed and drained

1 teaspoon dried onion flakes

8 flour or whole wheat tortillas (8" in diameter)

2 cups (8 ounces) shredded low-fat Colby or Monterey Jack cheese

1 cup salsa (optional)

½ cup fat-free sour cream (optional)

Place the beans and onion flakes in a small saucepan over low heat and cook for 5 minutes, or until warm. Mash the beans with a spoon. Keep warm.

Meanwhile, heat a large nonstick skillet coated with cooking spray over medium heat. Place 1 tortilla in the pan and sprinkle with ¼ cup of the cheese. Cook for 2 minutes, or until the cheese melts. Spoon one-quarter of the bean mixture on top and sprinkle with ¼ cup cheese. Top with another tortilla. Carefully turn the quesadilla and cook for 2 minutes, or until browned. Repeat to make a total of 4 quesadillas. Serve with the salsa and sour cream, if using.

Makes 4 quesadillas

Per quesadilla: *450 calories, 26 g protein, 57 g carbohydrates, 11 g fat, 10 mg cholesterol, 840 mg sodium, 3 g dietary fiber*

Diet Exchanges: *0 milk, 0 vegetable, 0 fruit, 4 bread, 2 meat, 1 fat*

Chicken Tacos with Salsa

239 Calories

3 limes
¼ cup orange juice
¼ cup chopped fresh cilantro
3 cloves garlic, minced
½ teaspoon ground cumin
4 boneless, skinless chicken breast halves, pounded to ½" thickness
1 large red onion, thinly sliced
6 whole wheat flour tortillas (8" diameter)
2 cups prepared salsa
¾ cup fat-free sour cream
2 cups finely shredded leaf lettuce

Grate the rind from the limes into a large bowl. Cut the limes in half and squeeze the juice into the bowl; discard the limes. Stir in the orange juice, cilantro, garlic, and cumin. Add the chicken and turn to coat. Cover and refrigerate for at least 1 hour or up to 4 hours; turn at least once while marinating.

Heat a large skillet coated with cooking spray over medium heat. Remove the chicken from the marinade; discard the marinade. Add the chicken and onion to the skillet and cook for 3 minutes per side, or until a thermometer inserted in the thickest portion registers 160°F and the juices run clear and the onions are softened. Cut the chicken into 1" slices.

Wrap the tortillas in plastic wrap and microwave on high power for 1 minute. Divide the chicken mixture among the tortillas. Top with the salsa, sour cream, and lettuce. Roll to enclose the filling. Slice each taco in half.

Makes 6 tacos

Per taco: *239 calories, 25 g protein, 37 g carbohydrates, 2 g fat, 45 mg cholesterol, 630 mg sodium, 5 g dietary fiber*

Diet Exchanges: *½ milk, 1½ vegetable, 0 fruit, 1 bread, 2½ meat, 0 fat*

Apricot Grilled Shrimp

223 Calories

1 cup apricot preserves

1 lemon

4 teaspoons soy sauce

2 cloves garlic, minced

2 teaspoons grated fresh ginger

1 teaspoon black pepper

2 pounds large shrimp, peeled and deveined

Place the preserves in a large microwaveable bowl. Microwave on high power for 30 seconds, or until melted. Grate 2 teaspoons rind from the lemon into the bowl. Cut the lemon in half and squeeze 2 tablespoons juice into the bowl. Stir in the soy sauce, garlic, ginger, and pepper. Add the shrimp and toss to coat. Cover and refrigerate for 30 minutes.

Coat a grill rack or broiler-pan rack with cooking spray. Preheat the grill or broiler.

Remove the shrimp from the marinade; reserve the marinade. Thread the shrimp onto 8 metal skewers, leaving $1/4$" between the pieces. Cook 4" from the heat, basting often with the marinade, for 2 minutes per side, or until the shrimp are opaque.

Place the remaining marinade in a saucepan and bring to a boil over medium-high heat. Cook for 2 minutes. Serve with the shrimp.

Makes 8 servings

Per serving: *223 calories, 24 g protein, 28 g carbohydrates, 2 g fat, 170 mg cholesterol, 400 mg sodium, 1 g dietary fiber*

Diet Exchanges: *0 milk, 0 vegetable, 0 fruit, $1^1/_2$ bread, $3^1/_2$ meat, 0 fat*

Kitchen Tip

If using bamboo skewers for this recipe, be sure to soak them in water for a few minutes before threading the shrimp on them so that they don't burn.

Succulent Grilled Salmon

—Ellen Curry, Benton, Illinois

"This is so incredibly easy to fix, and my kids and husband love it.
The marinade also works very well for other types of fish, so you can keep almost any
fish on hand and have a delicious entrée in less time than it takes to order pizza."

4 **salmon steaks (4 ounces each)**
¼ **cup ranch salad dressing**
   Cajun pepper seasoning, to taste
   Lemon slices (optional)

Place the salmon in a single layer in a large baking dish and cover with the dressing. Sprinkle with the Cajun seasoning. Marinate for 10 minutes, turning once.

Coat a grill rack with cooking spray. Preheat the grill.

Place the steaks on the prepared rack. Grill for 6 minutes, turning once, or until the fish is opaque. Serve with the lemon slices, if using.

Makes 4 servings

Per serving: *283 calories, 23 g protein, 1 g carbohydrates, 20 g fat, 70 mg cholesterol, 240 mg sodium, 0 g dietary fiber*

Diet Exchanges: *0 milk, 0 vegetable, 0 fruit, 0 bread, 3½ meat, 1 fat*

Grilled Eggplant

—**Monica Kempland, Edwardsville, Illinois**

"This allows me to meet my daily veggie requirements, and it's a savory summer grilled treat!"

1 medium eggplant
⅓ cup fat-free Italian dressing

Cut the eggplant into ½" slices and place in a shallow dish. Pour the dressing over the eggplant and marinate for up to 1 hour, turning occasionally to allow the dressing to completely cover the slices.

Coat a grill rack with cooking spray. Preheat the grill.

Remove the eggplant from the marinade and place on the grill rack. Cook for 7 minutes, turning once, or until slightly charred and tender.

Makes 4 servings

Per serving: *21 calories, 1 g protein, 5 g carbohydrates, 0 g fat, 0 mg cholesterol, 180 mg sodium, 1 g dietary fiber*

Diet Exchanges: *0 milk, 1 vegetable, 0 fruit, 0 bread, 0 meat, 0 fat*

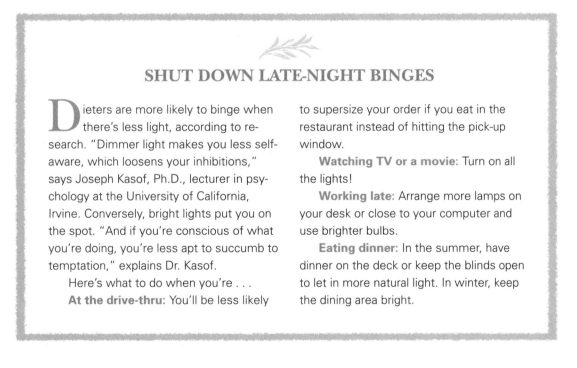

SHUT DOWN LATE-NIGHT BINGES

Dieters are more likely to binge when there's less light, according to research. "Dimmer light makes you less self-aware, which loosens your inhibitions," says Joseph Kasof, Ph.D., lecturer in psychology at the University of California, Irvine. Conversely, bright lights put you on the spot. "And if you're conscious of what you're doing, you're less apt to succumb to temptation," explains Dr. Kasof.

Here's what to do when you're . . .

At the drive-thru: You'll be less likely to supersize your order if you eat in the restaurant instead of hitting the pick-up window.

Watching TV or a movie: Turn on all the lights!

Working late: Arrange more lamps on your desk or close to your computer and use brighter bulbs.

Eating dinner: In the summer, have dinner on the deck or keep the blinds open to let in more natural light. In winter, keep the dining area bright.

Home-Run Hamburgers

3 tablespoons bulgur

⅓ cup boiling water

1 teaspoon olive oil

1 medium Vidalia onion, thinly sliced

1½ cups sliced shiitake mushrooms

1¼ pounds extra-lean ground beef

⅓ cup fresh bread crumbs

¼ cup chopped Italian parsley

2 tablespoons Worcestershire sauce

2 tablespoons tomato paste

2 cloves garlic, minced

1 teaspoon black pepper

½ teaspoon dry mustard

6 leaves red leaf lettuce

6 tomato slices

6 whole grain hamburger buns, split

Place the bulgur in a large bowl and add the water. Cover and let stand for 15 minutes, or until soft.

Heat the oil in a large nonstick skillet over medium heat. Add the onion and cook for 10 minutes, or until soft. Add the mushrooms and cook for 5 minutes, or until soft.

Drain the bulgur and return to the bowl. Stir in the beef, bread crumbs, parsley, Worcestershire sauce, tomato paste, garlic, pepper, and mustard. Shape the mixture into six 1"-thick patties.

Coat a grill rack or broiler-pan rack with cooking spray. Preheat the grill or broiler.

Cook the burgers 4" from the heat for 4 minutes per side, or until a thermometer inserted in a burger registers 160°F and the meat is no longer pink.

Place the lettuce and tomato on the bottom halves of the buns. Top with the burgers, then divide the onions and mushrooms among the burgers . Top each with the bun tops.

Makes 6 hamburgers

Per hamburger: *300 calories, 27 g protein, 36 g carbohydrates, 7 g fat, 50 mg cholesterol, 350 mg sodium, 6 g dietary fiber*

Diet Exchanges: *0 milk, 1½ vegetable, 0 fruit, 1½ bread, 3 meat, ½ fat*

Kitchen Tip

For hotter, smokier flavor, add a couple drops of liquid smoke and a few dashes of hot-pepper sauce to the meat mixture before forming into patties.

Portobello Burgers with Shoestring Fries

418 Calories

FRIES

2 egg whites

$\frac{1}{2}$ teaspoon paprika

$\frac{1}{4}$ teaspoon garlic powder

2 pounds baking potatoes, cut lengthwise into thin strips

BURGERS

1 hard-cooked egg white, finely chopped

2 tablespoons fat-free mayonnaise

1 tablespoon minced shallots

1 tablespoon chili sauce

1 teaspoon sweet pickle relish

8 medium portobello mushroom caps

Salt and black pepper

4 whole grain hamburger buns

4 leaves lettuce

8 tomato slices

To make the fries:

Preheat the oven to 425°F. Coat 2 baking sheets with cooking spray.

In a large bowl, combine the egg whites, paprika, and garlic powder. Add the potatoes and toss to coat. Place on the prepared baking sheets, allowing the excess egg whites to drain off. Bake for 15 minutes. Switch the position of the baking sheets and bake for 12 minutes longer, or until golden brown and crispy.

To make the burgers:

Coat a grill rack or broiler-pan rack with cooking spray. Preheat the grill or broiler.

In a small bowl, combine the egg white, mayonnaise, shallots, chili sauce, and relish. Coat the mushroom caps with cooking spray and season with salt and pepper. Cook 4" from the heat for 4 minutes per side, or until soft and tender. If desired, lightly toast the buns on the grill or under the broiler.

Place the lettuce leaves on the bottom halves of the buns. Top each with a mushroom cap. Place 2 tomato slices on each burger, then top with a second mushroom cap. Spread the seasoned mayonnaise on the bun tops and place on the burgers. Serve with the fries.

Makes 4 servings

Per serving: *418 calories, 17 g protein, 80 g carbohydrates, 2 g fat, 0 mg cholesterol, 450 mg sodium, 12 g dietary fiber*

Diet Exchanges: *0 milk, 5 vegetable, 0 fruit, $3\frac{1}{2}$ bread, $\frac{1}{2}$ meat, 0 fat*

Beef-Cabbage Casserole

—Carey Petersilka, Sturgeon Bay, Wisconsin

"I found this recipe especially good when I was trying to cut down on carbohydrates in my diet. I was a carb craver, and by cutting down on those in my diet, I was able to lose 38 pounds and have kept it off for 5 years!"

½ **head cabbage, cut into 6 wedges**

1½ **pounds lean ground beef**

½ **small onion, chopped**

½ **green bell pepper, chopped**

1 **can (28 ounces) diced tomatoes**

1 **teaspoon garlic salt**

¾ **cup (3 ounces) shredded low-fat Swiss cheese**

1 **teaspoon chopped parsley**

Bring 1" of salted water to a boil in a large saucepan over medium-high heat. Add the cabbage and cook for 15 minutes, or until tender. Drain and place in a 13" × 9" baking dish.

Meanwhile, heat a large skillet coated with cooking spray over medium-high heat. Add the beef and cook, stirring occasionally, for 10 minutes, or until browned. Drain and return to the skillet. Add the onion, pepper, tomatoes (with juice), and garlic salt and bring to a boil. Reduce the heat to low and cook, stirring occasionally, for 15 minutes, or until the vegetables are tender.

Preheat the oven to 350°F.

Pour the beef mixture over the cabbage and bake for 20 minutes. Sprinkle with the cheese and parsley and bake for 2 minutes longer, or until the cheese is melted.

Makes 8 servings

Per serving: *200 calories, 22 g protein, 9 g carbohydrates, 8 g fat, 34 mg cholesterol, 345 mg sodium, 3 g dietary fiber*

Diet Exchanges: *0 milk, 1½ vegetable, 0 fruit, 0 bread, 3 meat, ½ fat*

Chicken–Hash Brown Casserole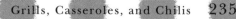

—Linda Laney-Rogers, Cabot, Arkansas

"This is a wonderful, easy, tasty dish that lets me give in to that creamy potato craving. The water chestnuts give it the crunch. It's so delicious, my granddaughters can eat half the dish by themselves!"

2 pounds frozen hash browns, thawed

4 cups cooked cubed chicken breast

4 ounces sliced mushrooms

1 can (5½ ounces) sliced water chestnuts

1 can (10¾ ounces) low-fat cream of chicken soup

1 can (14¾ ounces) fat-free chicken broth

1 cup fat-free sour cream

1 small onion, chopped

½ green bell pepper, chopped

1 clove garlic, minced

¼ teaspoon salt

¼ teaspoon ground black pepper

½ cup (2 ounces) shredded fat-free or reduced-fat extra-sharp Cheddar cheese

Preheat the oven to 350°F.

Squeeze any excess moisture from the hash browns and spread in a 13" × 9" baking dish. Top with the chicken, mushrooms, and water chestnuts.

In a large bowl, combine the soup, broth, sour cream, onion, bell pepper, garlic, salt, and black pepper. Pour over the chicken mixture.

Bake for 30 minutes. Top with the cheese and bake for 10 minutes, or until cooked through and bubbly.

Makes 8 servings

Per serving: *283 calories, 27 g protein, 35 g carbohydrates, 4 g fat, 55 mg cholesterol, 480 mg sodium, 3 g dietary fiber*

Diet Exchanges: *½ milk, 1 vegetable, 0 fruit, 1½ bread, 3 meat, ½ fat*

Chicken and Mushroom Pasta Casserole

8 ounces small rigatoni, cooked and drained

½ pound boneless, skinless chicken breast, patted dry

1 large portobello mushroom cap, cut in strips

1 onion, halved and sliced

2 cans (10 ounces each) low-fat, reduced-sodium condensed cream of mushroom soup

2 cups water

2 roasted red peppers, coarsely chopped

¼ cup chopped parsley

¼ teaspoon salt

⅓ cup (1½ ounces) grated Parmesan cheese

Preheat the oven to 375°F. Coat a 2-quart or 13" × 9" baking dish with cooking spray.

Prepare the pasta according to package directions.

Meanwhile, coat both sides of the chicken with cooking spray. Place in a large skillet over medium-high heat. Cook for 4 minutes per side, or until golden. Remove the chicken and set aside. Add the mushroom to the skillet and coat with cooking spray. Cook, stirring, for 5 minutes, or until soft. Remove and set aside with the chicken. Add the onion and coat with cooking spray. Cook, stirring, for 5 minutes, or until lightly golden.

Cut the chicken into strips and place in a large bowl. Add the mushroom, onion, pasta, soup, water, peppers, parsley, and salt. Stir to mix. Spoon into the prepared baking dish. Sprinkle with the Parmesan and cover loosely with foil. Bake for 20 minutes, or until hot and bubbly.

Makes 8 servings

Per serving: *209 calories, 14 g protein, 27 g carbohydrates, 5 g fat, 19 mg cholesterol, 173 mg sodium, 2 g dietary fiber*

Diet Exchanges: *0 milk, 1 vegetable, 0 fruit, 1½ bread, 1 meat, ½ fat*

Mexican Casserole

—Shontell Underdown, Fayetteville, Arkansas

"You can serve this dish with a can of corn sprinkled with black pepper."

2 cups broken low-fat corn chips

1 pound ground turkey breast

1 onion, chopped

1 can (10¾ ounces) low-fat cream of chicken soup

¾ cup salsa

¾ cup (3 ounces) shredded low-fat Cheddar cheese

Preheat the oven to 350°F. Place a layer of corn chips in an 11" × 7" baking dish.

Heat a large nonstick skillet over medium-high heat. Add the turkey and onion and cook, stirring frequently, for 5 minutes, or until the turkey is no longer pink and the onion is soft. Drain if necessary. Add the soup and salsa and stir to combine.

Place a layer of turkey over the chips in the baking dish and top with a layer of cheese and a layer of chips. Repeat to use the remaining turkey, cheese, and chips, ending with cheese.

Bake for 15 minutes, or until heated through. Let stand for 5 minutes before serving.

Makes 8 servings

Per serving: *170 calories, 14 g protein, 9 g carbohydrates, 9 g fat, 50 mg cholesterol, 425 mg sodium, 1 g dietary fiber*

Diet Exchanges: *0 milk, ½ vegetable, 0 fruit, ½ bread, 1½ meat, ½ fat*

THOUGHTFUL SNACKING

Snacks can tame your appetite and boost your energy—but don't overdo it!

According to a study of nearly 8,500 adults, we eat 26 percent more snack calories today than 15 years ago. What's more, snackers eat 560 more calories every day than nonsnackers. More frequent snacks, bigger portions, and more fattening choices are to blame.

But if you cut back to one 200-calorie snack a day, you could lose 38 pounds in a year. Stick to a 300-calorie snack and you'll still drop 27 pounds—without doing anything else. "Make snacks nutritious foods you miss during meals, such as fruits and yogurt," suggests study author Anna Maria Siega-Riz, R.D., Ph.D., assistant professor at the University of North Carolina at Chapel Hill.

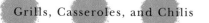

Tuna Casserole

—Charlotte Beachey, Kokomo, Indiana

*"I serve this dish with a salad and diet bread, and it's very filling.
If you like, you can brown the casserole under the broiler."*

1 **cup reduced-fat cottage cheese**

1 **small can (3 ounces) water-packed tuna, drained**

1 **small jar (4 ounces) mushrooms, drained**

1 **small onion, chopped**

1 **rib celery, chopped**

½ **red bell pepper, chopped**

Preheat the oven to 350°F. Coat a small baking dish with cooking spray.

Combine the cottage cheese, tuna, mushrooms, onion, celery, and bell pepper in the prepared baking dish. Bake for 30 minutes, or until golden.

Makes 2 servings

Per serving: *165 calories, 25 g protein, 13 g carbohydrates, 2 g fat, 15 mg cholesterol, 786 mg sodium, 3 g dietary fiber*

Diet Exchanges: *0 milk, 2 vegetable, 0 fruit, 0 bread, 3 meat, ½ fat*

Shrimp and Spinach Casserole

135 Calories

—Jennifer Lamontagne, Stratford, Connecticut

"I absolutely love seafood—it's low in calories and fat. Unfortunately, my husband isn't a big fan. This is one recipe that he doesn't complain about. The spinach is also an iron-rich, nutritious addition."

1 pound large shrimp, peeled, deveined, and quartered

1 package (10 ounces) frozen chopped spinach, thawed and squeezed dry

1 small yellow onion, chopped

¾ cup low-fat or fat-free mayonnaise

¼ cup (1 ounce) grated Parmesan cheese or soy substitute

1 tablespoon lemon juice

Pinch of ground red pepper

Ground black pepper, to taste

3 egg whites

½ teaspoon salt

Preheat the oven to 375°F. Coat a glass pie plate or gratin dish with cooking spray.

In a large bowl, combine the shrimp, spinach, onion, mayonnaise, cheese, lemon juice, red pepper, and black pepper.

Beat the egg whites in a medium bowl until stiff peaks form. Add to the shrimp mixture and sprinkle with the salt. Place in the prepared pie plate.

Bake for 40 minutes, or until browned and puffed and a knife inserted in the center comes out clean.

Makes 8 servings

Per serving: *135 calories, 16 g protein, 6 g carbohydrates, 6 g fat, 120 mg cholesterol, 480 mg sodium, 1 g dietary fiber*

Diet Exchanges: *0 milk, ½ vegetable, 0 fruit, 0 bread, 2 meat, 1 fat*

OUTSMART THE MARKETING

Nutrition scientists have found that high-calorie/low-nutrition foods like soft drinks, cakes, and ice cream gobble up 27 percent of all the calories that Americans eat. If you need to lose weight, zero in on the snacks you eat. Here's how:

Resist value marketing, which offers a supersize serving for just a little more money.

Avoid bringing junk food into the house. You'll be safe from temptation.

Always have a healthier alternative ready that looks appealing and helps satisfy your junk food craving.

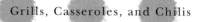

Garden Pasta Pie

—Barbara Meyers, Oregon, Ohio

442 Calories

"This is a great-tasting recipe to get your fresh spring vegetables into your daily diet plan. My husband and I have this at least a couple of times a month. He can't wait for the next sampling."

12 **ounces linguine**
1 **tablespoon olive oil**
1 **medium onion, chopped**
4 **cloves garlic, minced**
1 **tablespoon lemon juice**
2 **teaspoons dried oregano**
1½ **teaspoons dried basil**
¾ **teaspoon salt**
2 **cups part-skim ricotta cheese**
¼ **cup (1 ounce) grated Parmesan cheese**
2 **large eggs, lightly beaten**
2 **medium tomatoes, cored and sliced**
1 **medium zucchini, sliced and steamed**
½ **cup (2 ounces) shredded part-skim mozzarella cheese**
Fresh parsley sprigs (optional)

Preheat the oven to 375°F. Coat an 8" springform pan with cooking spray.

Prepare the pasta according to package directions. Drain and place in a serving bowl.

Meanwhile, heat the oil in a large skillet over medium heat. Add the onion and garlic and cook for 3 minutes, or until the onion is softened. Place in the bowl with the linguine, along with the lemon juice, 1 teaspoon of the oregano, ½ teaspoon of the basil, and the salt.

In another bowl, combine the ricotta, 2 tablespoons of the Parmesan, the eggs, the remaining 1 teaspoon oregano, and the remaining 1 teaspoon basil. Add to the linguine mixture and toss to combine.

Place half of the mixture in the prepared pan and top with half the tomatoes and half the zucchini. Add the remaining linguine mixture and top with the remaining tomatoes and zucchini. Sprinkle with the mozzarella and the remaining 2 tablespoons Parmesan. Cover with foil and place on a baking sheet.

Bake for 35 minutes. Remove the foil and bake for 5 minutes longer, or until hot and bubbly. Let stand for 10 minutes before cutting. Garnish with the parsley, if using.

Makes 6 servings

Per serving: *442 calories, 24 g protein, 54 g carbohydrates, 14 g fat, 105 mg cholesterol, 540 mg sodium, 3 g dietary fiber*

Diet Exchanges: *0 milk, 1 vegetable, 0 fruit, 3 bread, 2½ meat, 2 fat*

Vegetable Lasagna with Tofu

—Jennifer Suchorab, Prince Albert, Saskatchewan

"This lasagna has an abundance of flavor and utilizes soy, which is important for many aspects of health. My family loves it!"

8 ounces lasagna noodles

1 tablespoon olive oil

8 scallions, chopped

1 cup sliced button mushrooms

1 clove garlic, minced

1 package (10 ounces) frozen chopped spinach, thawed and squeezed dry

1 jar (48 ounces) spaghetti sauce

12 ounces firm tofu, drained and crumbled

1 egg

½ teaspoon dried oregano

½ teaspoon garlic powder

½ teaspoon salt

¼ teaspoon black pepper

2 cups (8 ounces) reduced-fat mozzarella cheese

Preheat the oven to 350°F.

Prepare the lasagna noodles according to package directions.

Meanwhile, heat the oil in a medium saucepan over medium-high heat. Add the scallions and mushrooms and cook, stirring, for 3 minutes, or until softened. Add the garlic and spinach and cook, stirring frequently, for 5 minutes, or until the vegetables are tender. Remove from the heat, stir in the spaghetti sauce, and set aside.

In a large bowl, combine the tofu, egg, oregano, garlic powder, salt, and pepper.

Spread 1 cup of the sauce mixture in a 13" × 9" baking dish. Place 3 lasagna noodles on top. Spread with 2 cups sauce, half of the tofu mixture, and ⅔ cup of the cheese. Repeat layering with the remaining noodles, sauce, and tofu mixture. Top with any remaining sauce mixture.

Cover with foil and bake for 45 minutes. Remove the foil, sprinkle with the remaining 1⅓ cups cheese, and bake, uncovered, for 15 minutes, or until hot and bubbly. Let stand for 10 minutes before serving.

Makes 8 servings

Per serving: *380 calories, 24 g protein, 44 g carbohydrates, 13 g fat, 40 mg cholesterol, 1,000 mg sodium, 7 g dietary fiber*

Diet Exchanges: *0 milk, 1 vegetable, 0 fruit, 3 bread, 2 meat, 1 fat*

Healthy and Delicious Spinach Lasagna

—Diane Smith, Carmel, Indiana

"This lasagna is great to make ahead of time. Just add a little water before putting it in the oven."

2 cups fat-free ricotta cheese

1 package (10 ounces) frozen chopped spinach, thawed and squeezed dry

1 egg or ¼ cup liquid egg substitute

1 teaspoon dried basil

½ teaspoon Italian seasoning

½ teaspoon salt

¼ teaspoon black pepper

2 cups (8 ounces) part-skim mozzarella cheese

1 jar (28 ounces) spaghetti sauce

6 whole wheat lasagna noodles

1 cup water

Preheat the oven to 350°F.

In a medium bowl, combine the ricotta, spinach, egg or egg substitute, basil, Italian seasoning, salt, pepper, and 1 cup of the mozzarella.

Evenly spread one-third of the sauce in a 13" × 9" baking dish. Top with 3 lasagna noodles. Spread half of the cheese mixture over the noodles. Repeat. Top with the remaining sauce and the remaining 1 cup mozzarella. Add the water around the corners of the baking dish. Cover tightly with foil.

Bake for 1 hour and 15 minutes, or until hot and bubbly.

Makes 8 servings

Per serving: *310 calories, 19 g protein, 27 g carbohydrates, 15 g fat, 59 mg cholesterol, 913 mg sodium, 3 g dietary fiber*

Diet Exchanges: *0 milk, ½ vegetable, 0 fruit, ½ bread, 2 meat, 1 fat*

— Kitchen Tip —

This recipe is extra-easy to prepare because you don't need to cook the noodles before layering them in the baking dish. The water in the recipe provides the liquid needed to cook the noodles.

Five-Star Vegetable Chili

341 Calories

1 teaspoon olive oil

1 onion, chopped

1 green bell pepper, chopped

2 cloves garlic, minced

1 jalapeño chile pepper, minced (wear plastic gloves when handling), optional

1 tablespoon dried oregano

2 teaspoons chili powder

1 teaspoon ground cumin

1 can (28 ounces) no-salt-added diced tomatoes

1 can (15 ounces) no-salt-added tomato sauce

2 cups water

½ cup bulgur

2 cans (14–19 ounces each) beans, such as cannellini and/or kidney beans, rinsed and drained

Warm the oil in a Dutch oven over medium heat. Add the onion and bell pepper and cook, stirring occasionally, for 5 minutes, or until softened. Add the garlic, chile pepper, oregano, chili powder, and cumin and cook for 2 minutes.

Add the tomatoes (with juice), tomato sauce, and water. Increase the heat to medium-high and cook, stirring occasionally, for 5 minutes. Stir in the bulgur and beans. Reduce the heat to medium and cook for 15 minutes, or until thickened.

Makes 4 servings

Per serving: *341 calories, 14 g protein, 66 g carbohydrates, 3 g fat, 0 mg cholesterol, 430 mg sodium, 19 g dietary fiber*

Diet Exchanges: *0 milk, 4½ vegetable, 0 fruit, 2½ bread, 0 meat, ½ fat*

GREAT GO-ALONG

Serve homemade cornbread with this hearty chili for a family-pleasing, healthy helping of lycopene—a phytochemical that helps prevent disease—and extra dietary fiber. Mix 1 cup cornmeal, ½ cup unbleached all-purpose flour, 1 tablespoon sugar, 1½ teaspoons baking powder, 1 teaspoon baking soda, and ½ teaspoon salt.

Then mix 1 cup buttermilk, ½ cup liquid egg substitute, ⅓ cup sour cream, 2 tablespoons canola oil, ½ cup frozen corn kernels, and 2 ounces reduced-fat Cheddar. Combine both mixtures, then pour into a 9" × 9" baking dish coated with cooking spray. Bake at 400°F for about 25 minutes. Only 123 calories and 4 grams fat!

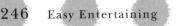

Very Veggie Chili

—Cynthia Moulthrop, Spring Hill, Tennessee

"The vegetables and meat substitute fill me up and provide some of my five daily servings of vegetables while being low in fat and high in fiber. And it tastes good!"

8 ounces sliced mushrooms
1 onion, chopped
1 red bell pepper, chopped
1 green bell pepper, chopped
2 cans (14½ ounces each) diced tomatoes
2 cans (14–19 ounces each) chili beans in sauce
1 bag frozen veggie crumbles
1 tablespoon chili powder
1 teaspoon ground cumin
1 cup (4 ounces) low-fat shredded sharp Cheddar cheese

Heat a large saucepan coated with cooking spray over medium-high heat. Add the mushrooms, onion, and bell peppers and cook, stirring frequently, for 5 minutes, or until the vegetables are tender. Add the tomatoes, beans, veggie crumbles, chili powder, and cumin. Bring to a boil, reduce the heat to medium, and simmer for 20 minutes to blend the flavors. Serve sprinkled with the cheese.

Makes 6 servings

Per serving: *200 calories, 17 g protein, 19 g carbohydrates, 7 g fat, 15 mg cholesterol, 690 mg sodium, 5 g dietary fiber*

Diet Exchanges: *0 milk, 2½ vegetable, 0 fruit, 0 bread, 2 meat, ½ fat*

SECRETS OF WEIGHT-LOSS WINNERS

• I joined TOPS (Take Off Pounds Sensibly). This group approach has been the motivation I sorely needed. I'm now the leader of my group of about 35 ladies and gentlemen.

—Barbara Meyers, Oregon, Ohio

• The Inches-A-Weigh program taught me how to sensibly eat what I like and exercise my problem areas. I took off 40 pounds and six dress sizes!

—Donna Vomachka, Springfield, Illinois

Festive Menus

Whether you're having a family dinner or just having friends over for a casual get-together, a little planning can go a long way, especially if you're trying to lose weight. Some of these special-occasion menus may be a little higher in calories than your everyday weeknight meals, but as long as you keep portions in check, there's no reason why you can't enjoy the fun—and the food—along with everyone else. Try these menus as they are, pick and choose dishes from several different menus, or create all new ones by incorporating your own healthy home-made favorites.

Each menu includes a one-serving nutritional analysis so you can easily work them into your daily eating plan. The portion size for all the recipes listed is one serving.

Ladies' Day Lunch

Shrimp and Spinach Casserole, page 240

Hoppin' John Salad, page 166

Yogurt Parfaits, page 76

Per serving: 600 calories, 60 g protein, 67 g carbohydrates, 12 g fat, 130 mg cholesterol, 940 mg sodium, 8 g dietary fiber

Diet Exchanges: ½ milk, 2½ vegetable, 0 fruit, 3 bread, 5½ meat, 2 fat

Outdoor Elegance

Apricot Grilled Shrimp, page 227

Grilled Eggplant, page 229

Favorite Bean Salad, page 168

Frozen Fruit Dessert, page 77

Per serving: 518 calories, 33 g protein, 93 g carbohydrates, 4 g fat, 170 mg cholesterol, 760 mg sodium, 10 g dietary fiber

Diet Exchanges: 0 milk, 2 vegetable, 2 fruit, 2 bread, 3½ meat, 0 fat

Fun in the Sun

Home-Run Hamburgers, page 230

French Oven Fries, page 134

Fabulous 5-Minute Coleslaw, page 163

Lemon Mini Tarts, page 43

Per serving: 670 calories, 39 g protein, 112 g carbohydrates, 13 g fat, 50 mg cholesterol, 1,095 mg sodium, 15 g dietary fiber

Diet Exchanges: 0 milk, 2½ vegetable, 0 fruit, 5½ bread, 3½ meat, 1½ fat

Potluck Portables

Roasted Veggie Dip, page 211

Healthy and Delicious Spinach Lasagna, page 243

Gold Rush Lemon Bars, page 45

Per serving: 414 calories, 21 g protein, 45 g carbohydrates, 18 g fat, 64 mg cholesterol, 948 mg sodium, 3 g dietary fiber

Diet Exchanges: 0 milk, ½ vegetable, 0 fruit, 1½ bread, 2 meat, 1½ fat

Kid Pleasers

Easy Chicken and Vegetable Pizza, page 220

Orange Skimsicle, page 208

Walnut Brownies, page 46

Per serving: 592 calories, 27 g protein, 69 g carbohydrates, 25 g fat, 70 mg cholesterol, 550 mg sodium, 4 g dietary fiber

Diet Exchanges: 0 milk, 1½ vegetable, 1 fruit, 3 bread, 2½ meat, 4½ fat

Chesapeake Bay Supper

Crab Cakes with Roasted Pepper Sauce, page 125

Sweet Potato Fries, page 134

Lite Banana Cream Pie, page 62

Per serving: 522 calories, 29 g protein, 70 g carbohydrates, 15 g fat, 115 mg cholesterol, 1,026 mg sodium, 6 g dietary fiber

Diet Exchanges: 0 milk, 1 vegetable, ½ fruit, 3 bread, 3½ meat, 2 fat

Tex-Mex Tonight

Black Bean Soup, page 155

Chicken Tacos with Salsa, page 224

Chocolate-Raspberry Cooler, page 76

Per serving: 605 calories, 49 g protein, 96 g carbohydrates, 6 g fat, 55 mg cholesterol, 1,530 mg sodium, 13 g dietary fiber

Diet Exchanges: 1½ milk, 2½ vegetable, 0 fruit, 3½ bread, 4 meat, 1 fat

A Taste of Italy

Italian Mushroom Soup, page 159

Susan's Sweet 'n' Spicy Tomato-Basil Pasta, page 187

Tiramisu, page 71

Per serving: 642 calories, 18 g protein, 113 g carbohydrates, 15 g fat, 78 mg cholesterol, 1,401 mg sodium, 7 g dietary fiber

Diet Exchanges: 0 milk, 3½ vegetable, 0 fruit, 6 bread, ½ meat, 1½ fat

Dinner by Candlelight

Easy Creamy Pink Salmon, page 126

Stuffed Vidalia Onions, page 140

Fruit 'n' Spinach Salad, page 161

Chocolate Mousse, page 74

Per serving: 689 calories, 50 g protein, 79 g carbohy-drates, 20 g fat, 120 mg cholesterol, 710 mg sodium, 14 g dietary fiber

Diet Exchanges: 0 milk, 5 1/2 vegetable, 1/2 fruit, 2 1/2 bread, 6 meat, 3 1/2 fat

Sunday Supper

Herb-Crusted Leg of Lamb, page 85

Asparagus Medley, page 139

Potatoes Peperonata, page 132

Pineapple Angel Food Cake, page 48

Per serving: 678 calories, 36 g protein, 85 g car-bohydrates, 22 g fat, 70 mg cholesterol, 1,520 mg sodium, 6 g dietary fiber

Diet Exchanges: 0 milk, 1 vegetable, 1 fruit, 4 bread, 4 meat, 2 1/2 fat

The Big Game

All-Purpose Garlic Dip, page 213, with sliced raw vegetables

Five-Star Vegetable Chili, page 245

Cornbread, page 245

Chocolate Chippers, page 40

Per serving: 592 calories, 22 g protein, 99 g carbohydrates, 13 g fat, 24 mg cholesterol, 977 mg sodium, 20 g dietary fiber

Diet Exchanges: 0 milk, 4$\frac{1}{2}$ vegetable, 0 fruit, 4$\frac{1}{2}$ bread, $\frac{1}{2}$ meat, 2 fat

Be My Valentine

Scallops in Citrus Marinade, page 94

Brown Rice with Peppers and Zucchini, page 182

Sweetheart Cherry Pie, page 59

Per serving: 678 calories, 36 g protein, 85 g carbohydrates, 22 g fat, 70 mg cholesterol, 1,520 mg sodium, 6 g dietary fiber

Diet Exchanges: 0 milk, 1 vegetable, 1 fruit, 4 bread, 4 meat, 2$\frac{1}{2}$ fat

Photography Credits

Front Cover

Kurt Wilson/Rodale Images (cinnamon roll, chicken pesto pizza, chocolate cake)
Tad Ware & Company Inc./Rodale Images (beef stew)
Mitch Mandel/Rodale Images (shrimp pasta)

Back Cover

Courtesy of Ann Hirschy (before, after)
Mitch Mandel/Rodale Images (chocolate mousse, hamburger, chicken and vegetable couscous)

Interior

Mitch Mandel/Rodale Images: pages vii, 33, 38, 44, 50, 61, 64, 69, 70, 75, 83, 84, 89, 98, 101, 104, 114, 119, 121, 123, 124, 133, 141, 151, 154, 158, 163, 171, 175, 176, 181, 184, 189, 190, 196, 204, 207, 214, 218, 225, 227, 231, 232, 244, 248 (shrimp), 249, 250 (crab cakes), 251, 252, 253 (chili)

Tad Ware & Company Inc./Rodale Images: pages 58, 107, 129, 253 (pie)

Kurt Wilson/Rodale Images: pages 10, 11, 12, 13, 14, 15, 16, 17, 21, 26, 47, 53, 66, 79, 109, 130, 144, 167, 193, 203, 212, 217, 237, 248 (hoppin' John salad)

Rodale Images: pages 41, 80, 92, 250 (brownies)

© EyeWire Collection: page 18

© Artville: pages 26, 32, 34

© Brian Hagiwara: page 25

Courtesy of Ann Hirschy: page 49

Courtesy of Debra Whitfield: page 72

Courtesy of Ann & Butch Painter: page 87

Courtesy of Jennifer Jensen: page 95

Courtesy of Kelly Jens (before): page 103

Eric Francis/Liaison Agency (after): page 103

Courtesy of Lucini Vinegar: page 136

Courtesy of Jennifer Hoffmann: page 153

Courtesy of Melissa's Laptop Salads: page 165

Courtesy of Carole DeMartino (before): page 179

Mike Peters/Liaison Agency (after): page 179

Courtesy of Millie Wiley: page 195

Courtesy of Ron Burke (before): page 215

Edwin H. Remsberg/Liaison Agency (after): page 215

Courtesy of Lori LaRizzio (before): page 222

Troy Schnyder Photography (after): page 222

Index

Boldface page references indicate photographs. <u>Underscored</u> references indicate boxed text.

H

I

J

K

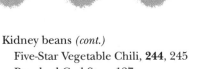

Conversion Chart

These equivalents have been slightly rounded to make measuring easier.

VOLUME MEASUREMENTS

U.S.	Imperial	Metric
¼ tsp	–	1 ml
½ tsp	–	2 ml
1 tsp	–	5 ml
1 Tbsp	–	15 ml
2 Tbsp (1 oz)	1 fl oz	30 ml
¼ cup (2 oz)	2 fl oz	60 ml
⅓ cup (3 oz)	3 fl oz	80 ml
½ cup (4 oz)	4 fl oz	120 ml
⅔ cup (5 oz)	5 fl oz	160 ml
¾ cup (6 oz)	6 fl oz	180 ml
1 cup (8 oz)	8 fl oz	240 ml

WEIGHT MEASUREMENTS

U.S.	Metric
1 oz	30 g
2 oz	60 g
4 oz (¼ lb)	115 g
5 oz (⅓ lb)	145 g
6 oz	170 g
7 oz	200 g
8 oz (½ lb)	230 g
10 oz	285 g
12 oz (¾ lb)	340 g
14 oz	400 g
16 oz (1 lb)	455 g
2.2 lb	1 kg

LENGTH MEASUREMENTS

U.S.	Metric
¼"	0.6 cm
½"	1.25 cm
1"	2.5 cm
2"	5 cm
4"	11 cm
6"	15 cm
8"	20 cm
10"	25 cm
12" (1')	30 cm

PAN SIZES

U.S.	Metric
8" cake pan	20 × 4 cm sandwich or cake tin
9" cake pan	23 × 3.5 cm sandwich or cake tin
11" × 7" baking pan	28 × 18 cm baking tin
13" × 9" baking pan	32.5 × 23 cm baking tin
15" × 10" baking pan	38 × 25.5 cm baking tin (Swiss roll tin)
1½ qt baking dish	1.5 liter baking dish
2 qt baking dish	2 liter baking dish
2 qt rectangular baking dish	30 × 19 cm baking dish
9" pie plate	22 × 4 or 23 × 4 cm pie plate
7" or 8" springform pan	18 or 20 cm springform or loose-bottom cake tin
9" × 5" loaf pan	23 × 13 cm or 2 lb narrow loaf tin or pâté tin

TEMPERATURES

Fahrenheit	Centigrade	Gas
140°	60°	–
160°	70°	–
180°	80°	–
225°	105°	¼
250°	120°	½
275°	135°	1
300°	150°	2
325°	160°	3
350°	180°	4
375°	190°	5
400°	200°	6
425°	220°	7
450°	230°	8
475°	245°	9
500°	260°	–